BE… …RSET

Stretching from the elegant Georgian town of Lyme Regis in the west to the bustling resort of Bournemouth in the east, Dorset has a rich variety of attractions. The impressive coastline, with its many well-known resorts, is indented with sandy coves and fine beaches and in many places the cliffs have been carved into dramatic shapes by the relentless action of the wind and sea. Inland is the heathland and pastoral scenery so beloved of Thomas Hardy and vividly portrayed in his novels as the county of Wessex. Set amid the vast panoramas of Blackmore Vale and Cranborne Chase, historic market towns and ancient villages testify to the rich heritage of the county.

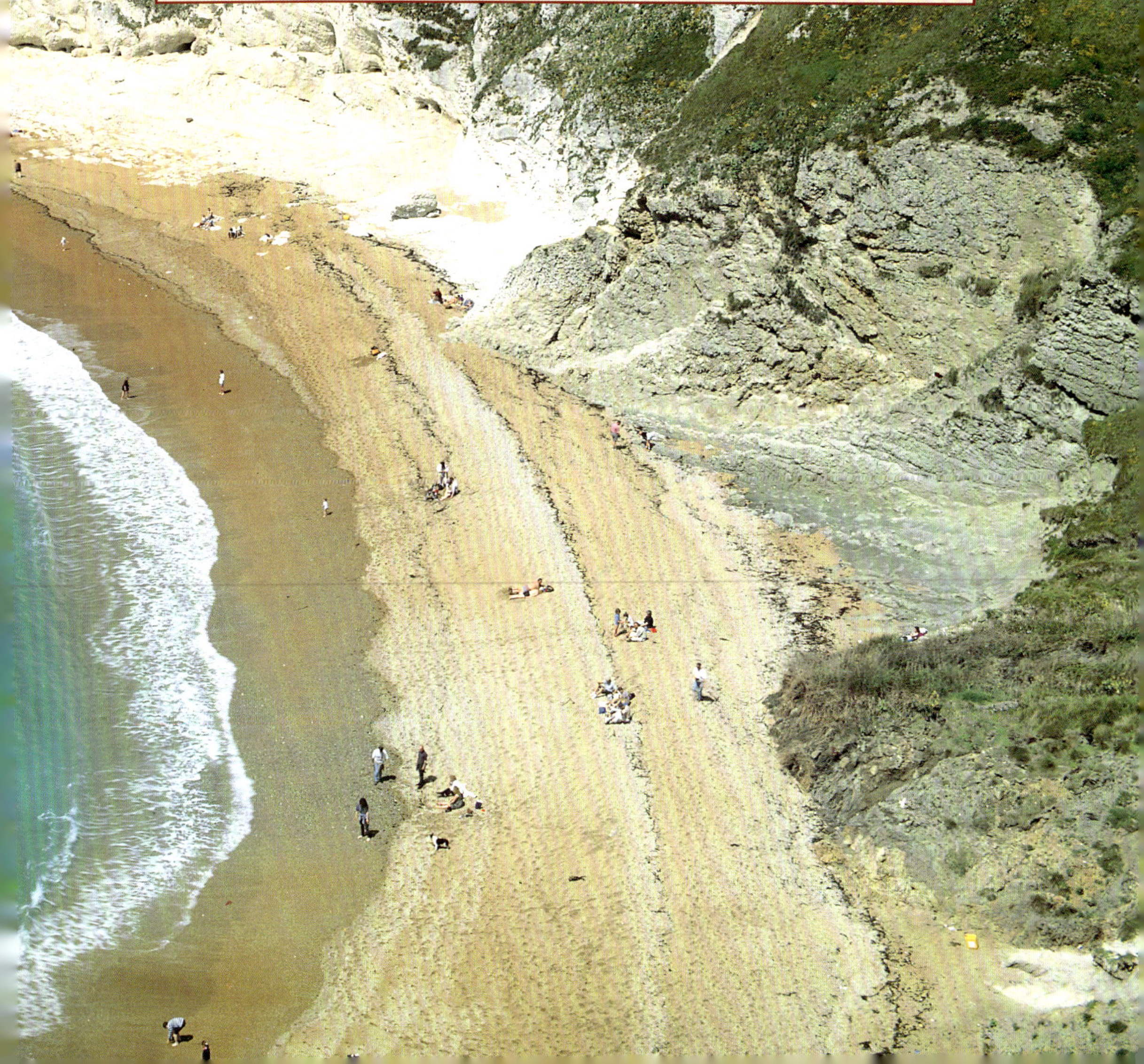

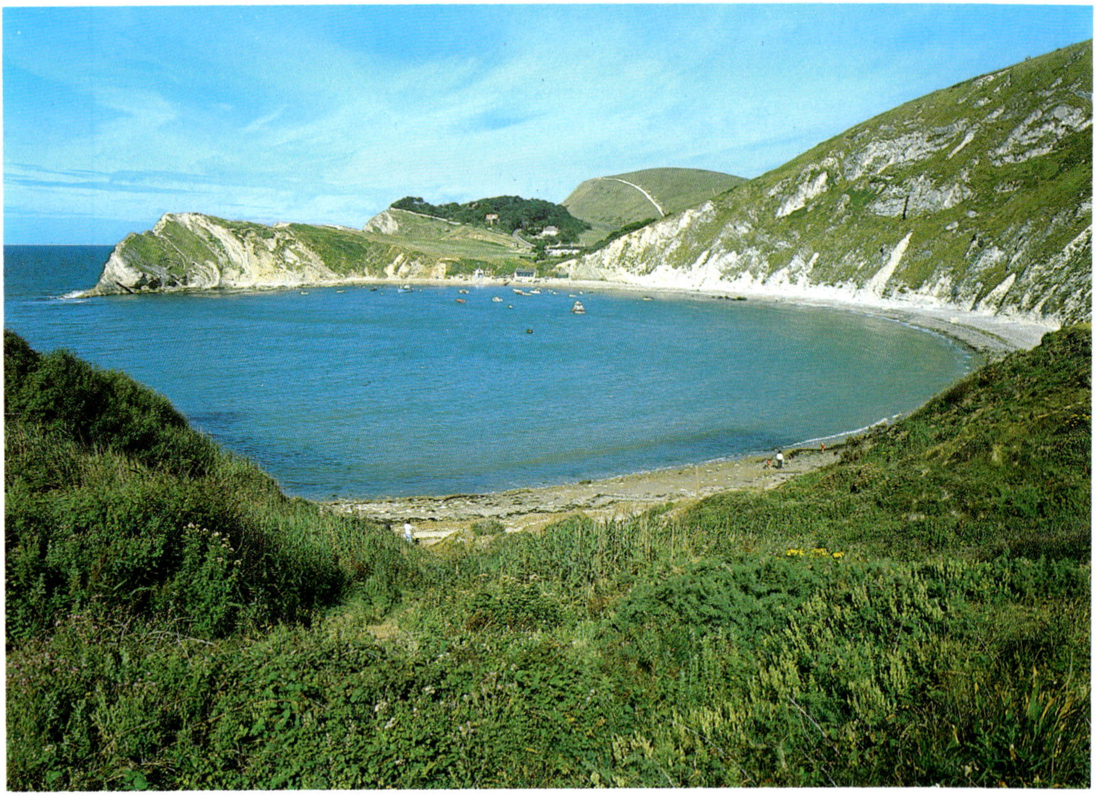

Lulworth Cove

Durdle Door

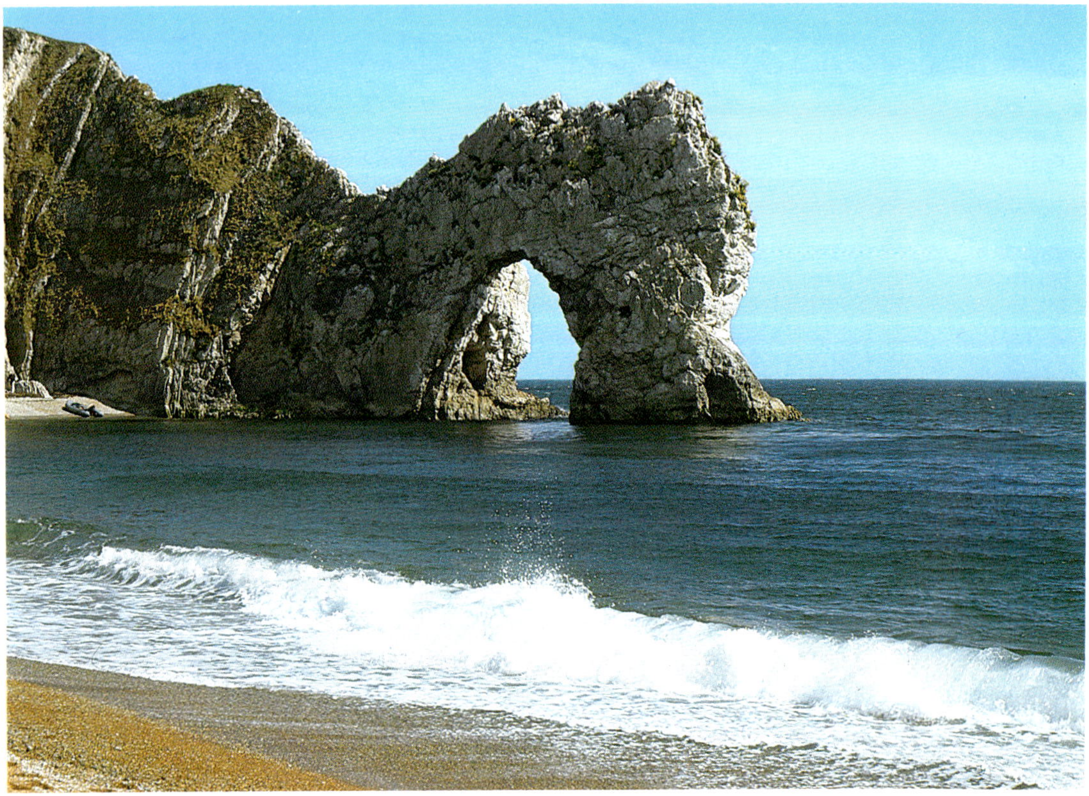

Lulworth Cove is a small and almost land-locked bay backed by towering cliffs nearly 400 feet high. It has a very narrow exit to the sea and was created by the action of the waves breaking through the stone and wearing away the softer clay behind it The beach is pebble but both bathing and boating are popular and from the cliff top there are fine views of some of the most outstanding coastal scenery in the county. To the west of Lulworth Cove there is a fascinating area of coves and cliff formations. The magnificent caves found at **Stair Hole** include Cathedral Cavern where pillars of rock rise from the sea to support the roof. Beyond is the spectacular natural rock arch which is known as **Durdle Door.** It stands 40 feet high and was formed by the sea eroding the softer rocks to leave the harder Portland stone. Its name comes from the Anglo-Saxon word "thirl", meaning "to pierce".

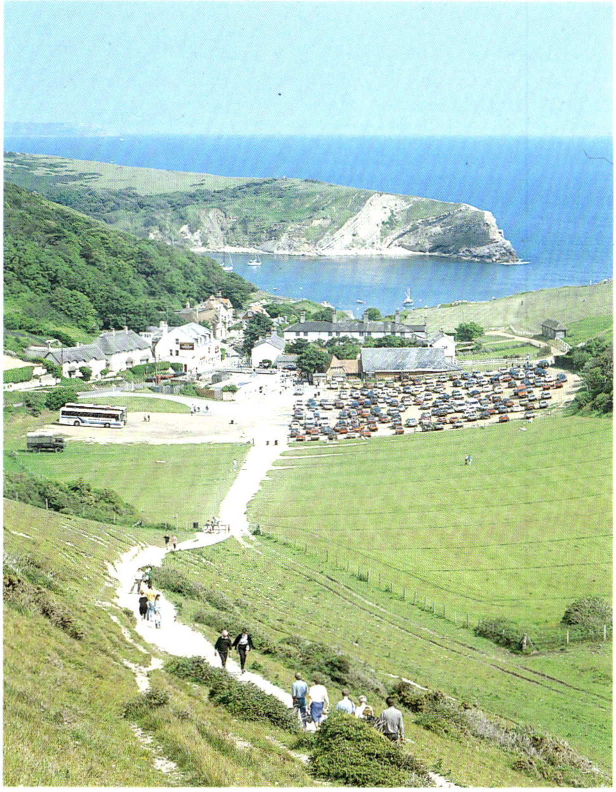

Lulworth Cove

The Stair Hole

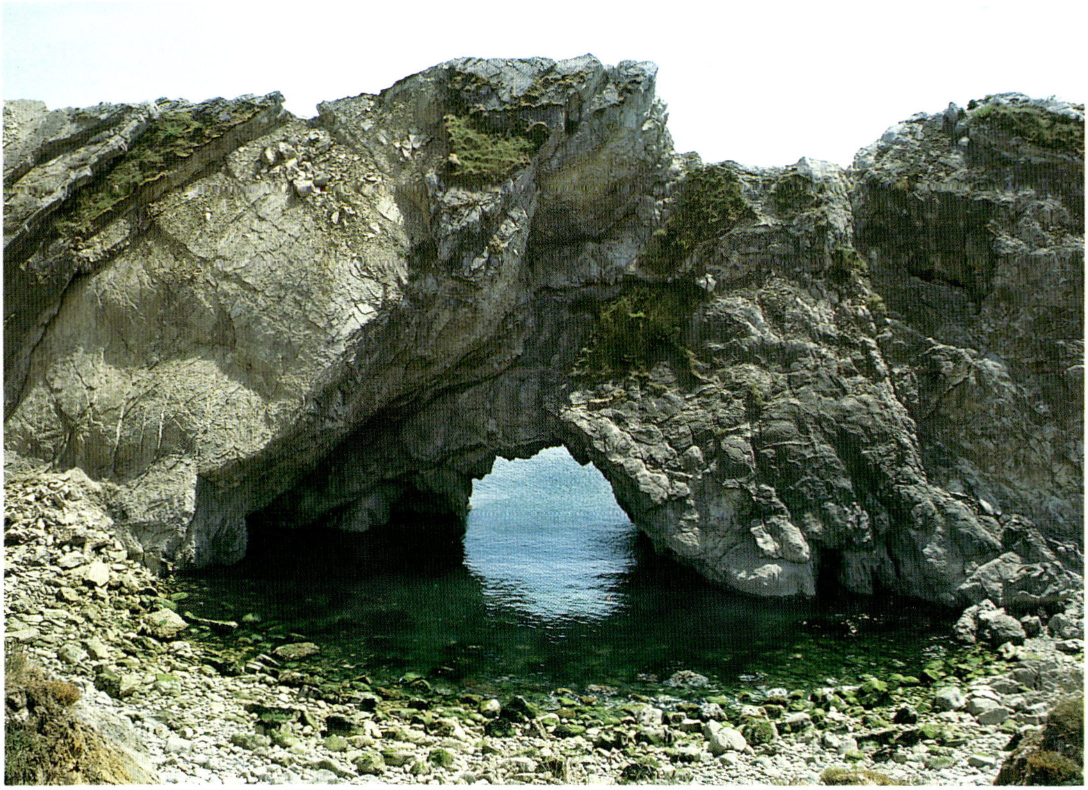

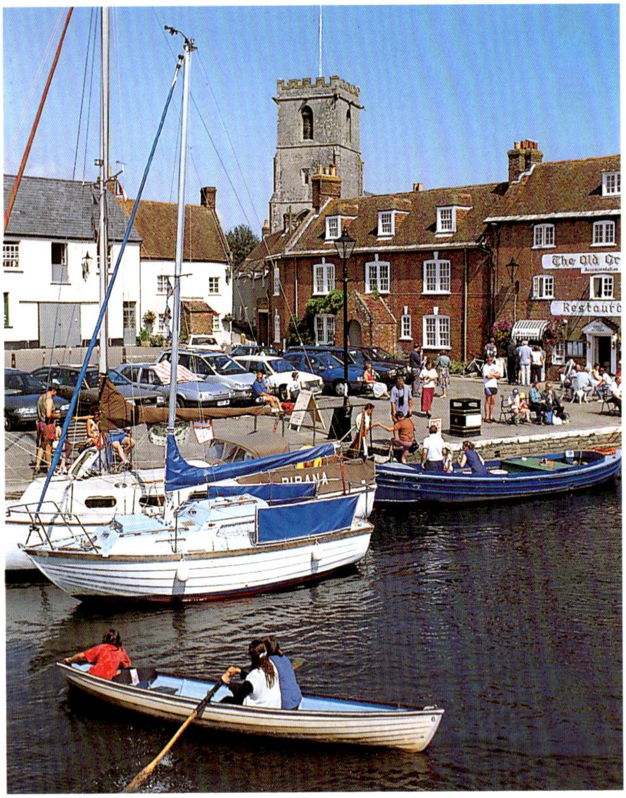

The Quay, Wareham

Dominated by the majestic ruins of its castle, the village of **Corfe Castle** is situated strategically in a gap in the Purbeck Hills. This ancient site was probably first fortified by King Alfred as a defence against the Danes. The present Norman castle was a formidable fortress with six towers in addition to the two which flank the Gate Tower. During the Civil War it was beseiged by the Roundhead forces after which the castle was largely demolished, much of the stone going to build houses in the village. **Wareham** is a delightful old town on the River Frome with wide streets, fine churches and some picturesque inns. On its way from Wareham to Corfe, the road crosses open,sandy heathland and nearby, amid the pine trees, is the famous **Blue Pool**. This attractive lake occupies the site of an old clay pit which accounts for the wonderful blue colour of the water from which the pool takes its name.

The Blue Pool

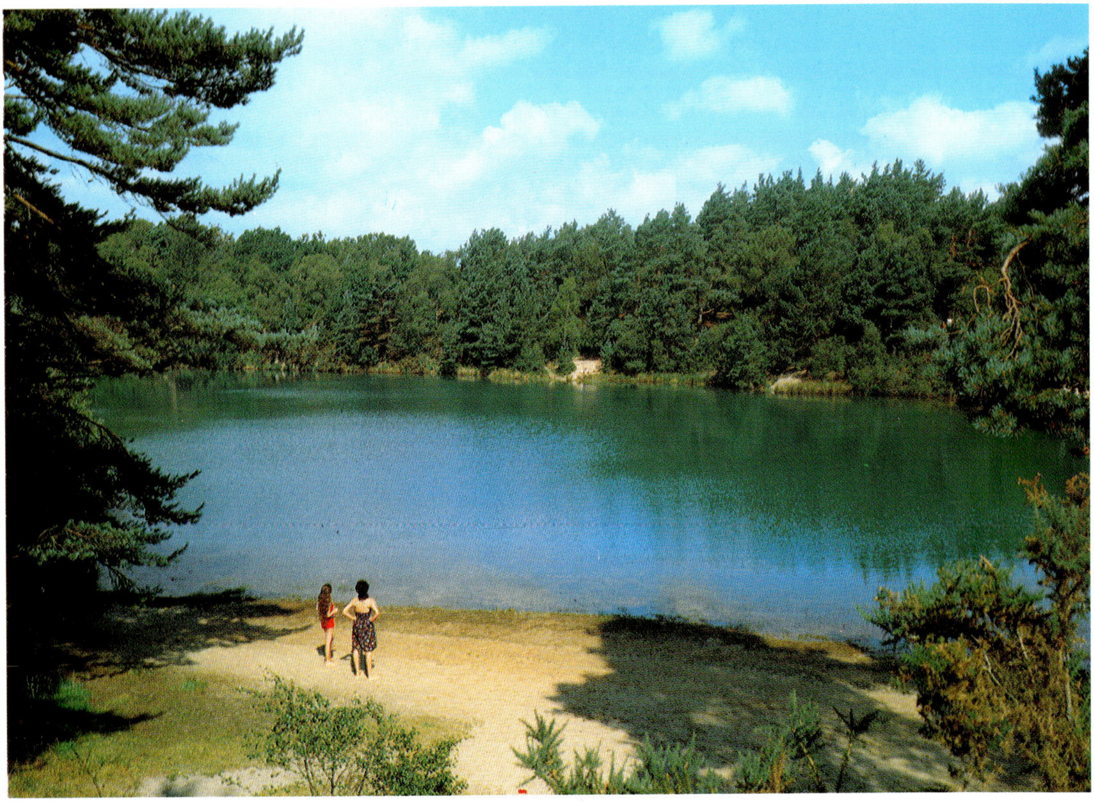

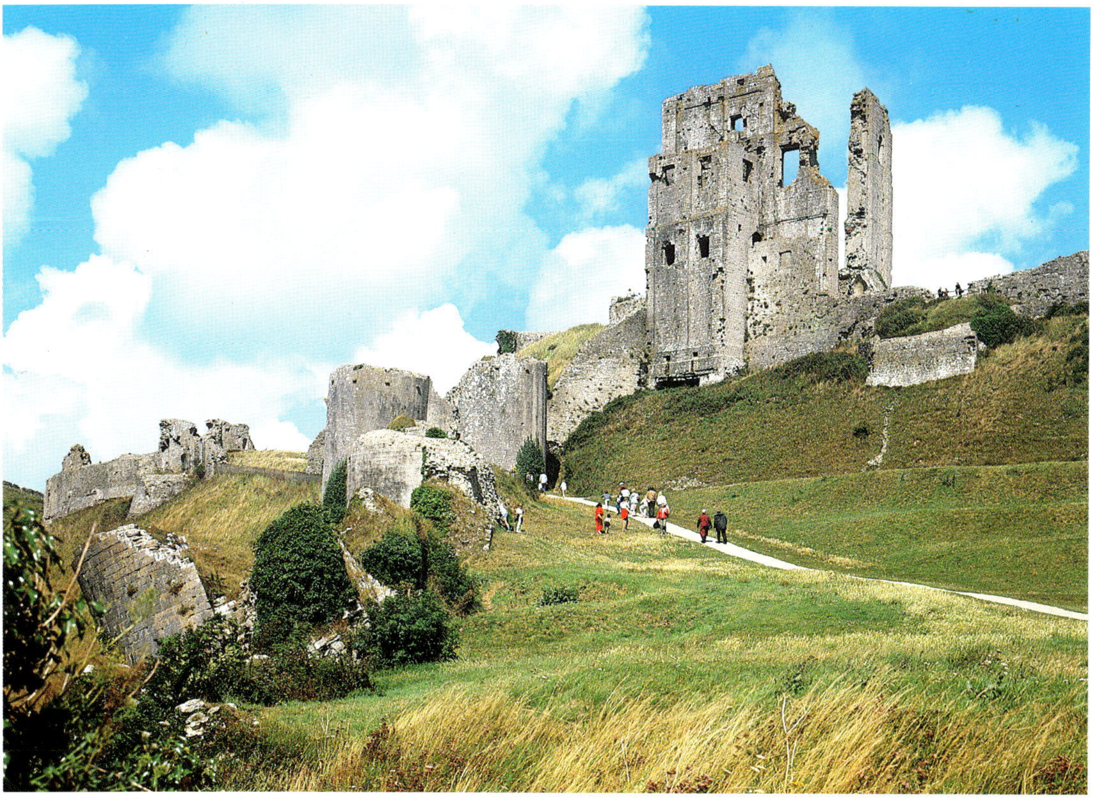

Corfe Castle from the Lower Ward

Corfe Castle from the Church

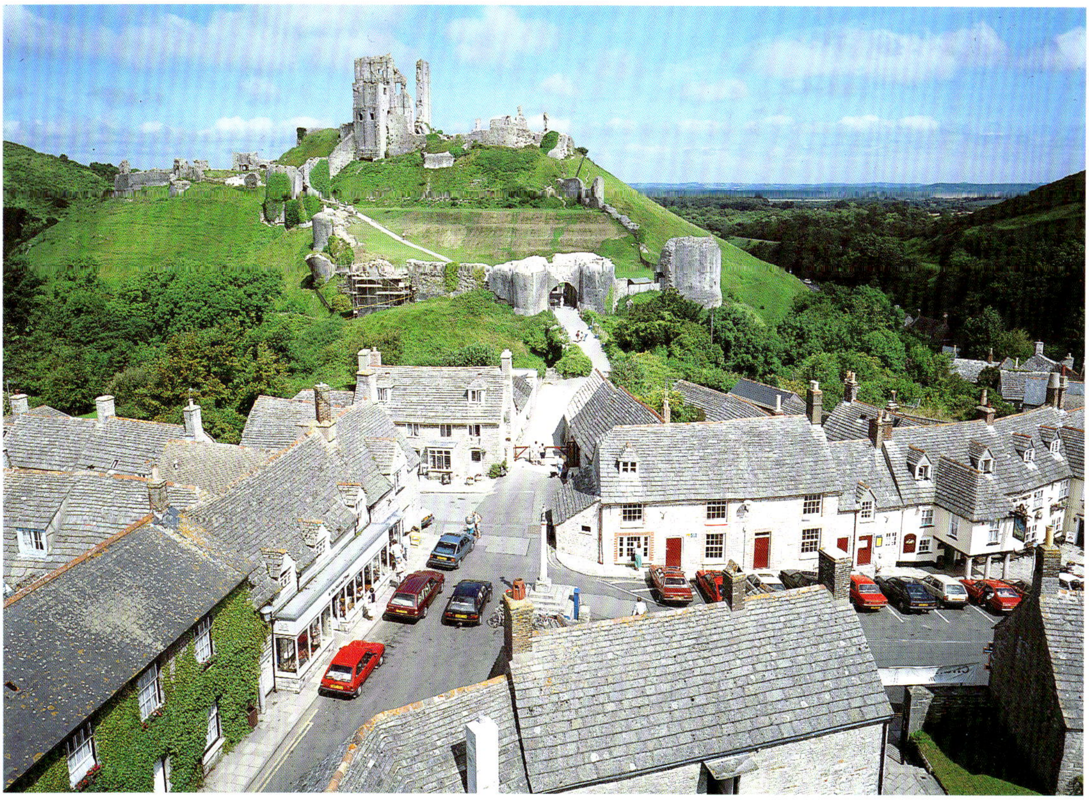

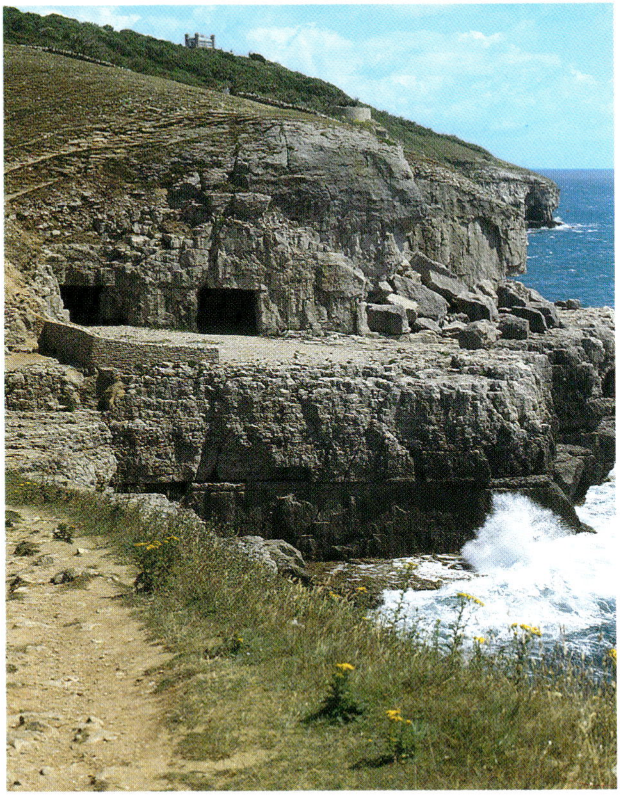

Tilly Whim Caves

A short way to the south of Swanage, between Durlston Head and Anvil Point, are the well known **Tilly Whim Caves,** part of a long disused underground stone quarry. **Anvil Point,** where the sea tears at the rugged cliffs, derives its name from the anvil-shaped rock which can be seen just off the coast.

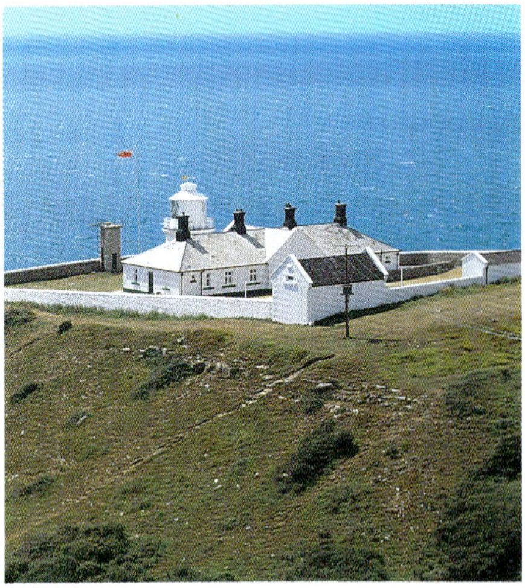

Anvil Point

The **Great Globe**, is located at Durlston Head in the Durlston Country Park a mile south of Swanage. This massive sphere is carved from Portland stone, weighs forty tons and measures ten feet in diameter. The earth's features are carved in relief on the surface of the globe which is placed to represent the position of the earth in space. Nearby there are some stone slabs which provide information about the earth, sun, moon and stars. The globe, which was first placed here in 1887 by Swanage-born builder John Mowlem, is one of the unusual attractions in the locality.

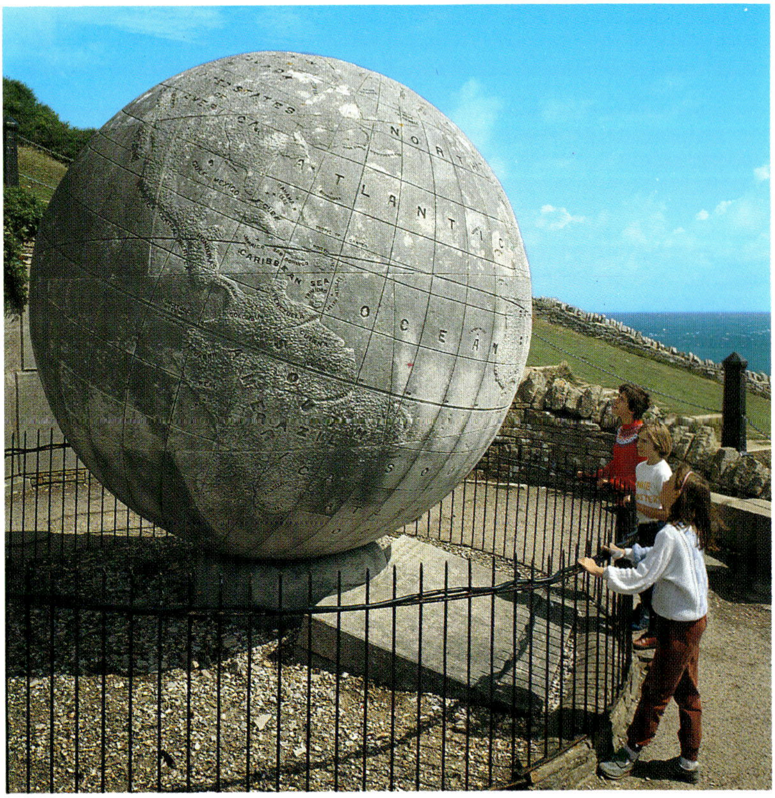

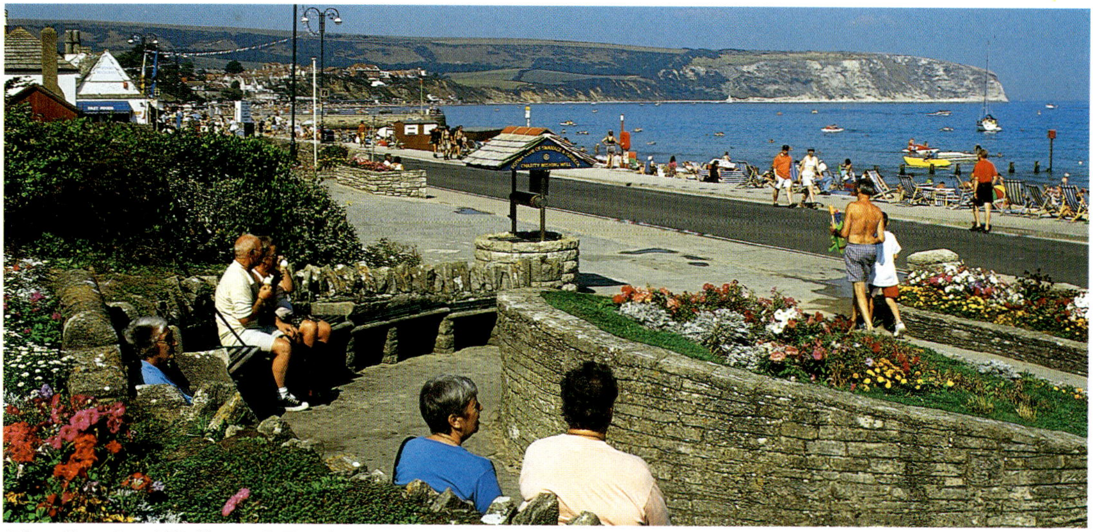

The Garden Walk and Esplanade

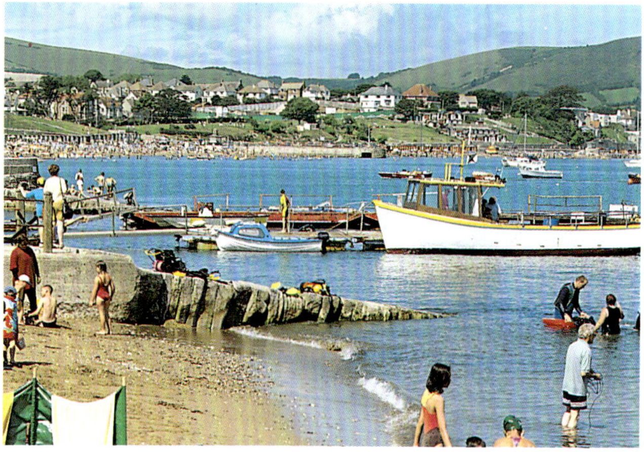

The Sands

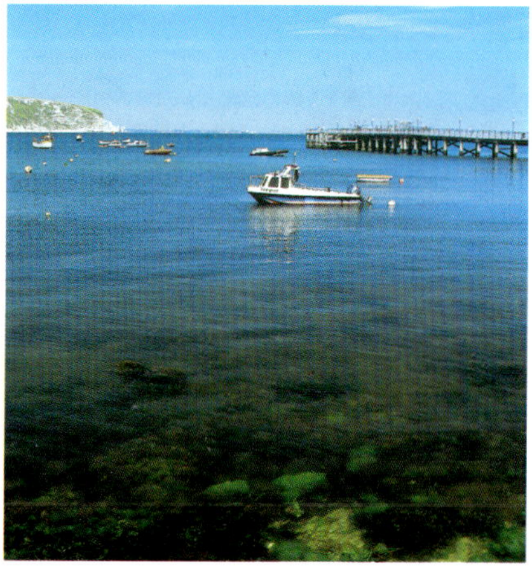

The Pier

The Mill Pond

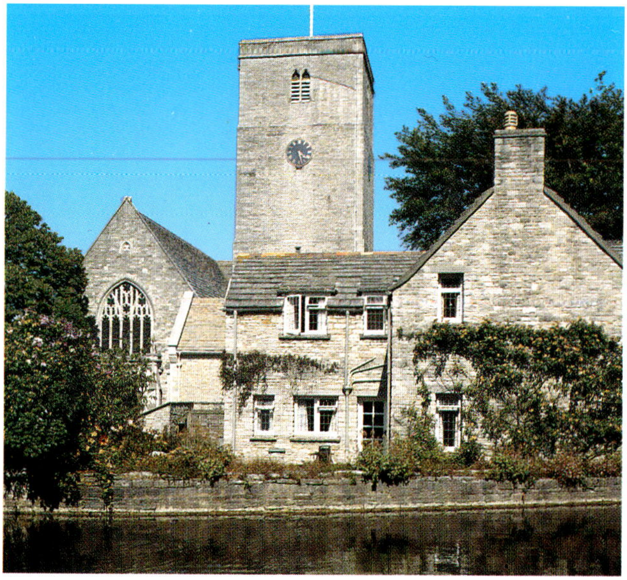

Swanage, once the chief centre of the Purbeck limestone quarrying industry, is today a very popular holiday resort. The lively sea-front esplanade extends for nearly a mile and the pier provides two landing stages as well as seats and shelters. Swanage lies at the southern end of a semi-circular sandy bay, the southernmost tip of which is low lying Peveril Point. It is sheltered to the north by the great rounded bulk of Ballard Down with its high chalk cliffs. Originally Swanage was little more than a tiny village inhabited by quarrymen and fisherfolk. Today one of the prettiest relics of the old village is the tiny Mill Pond, surrounded by stone cottages.

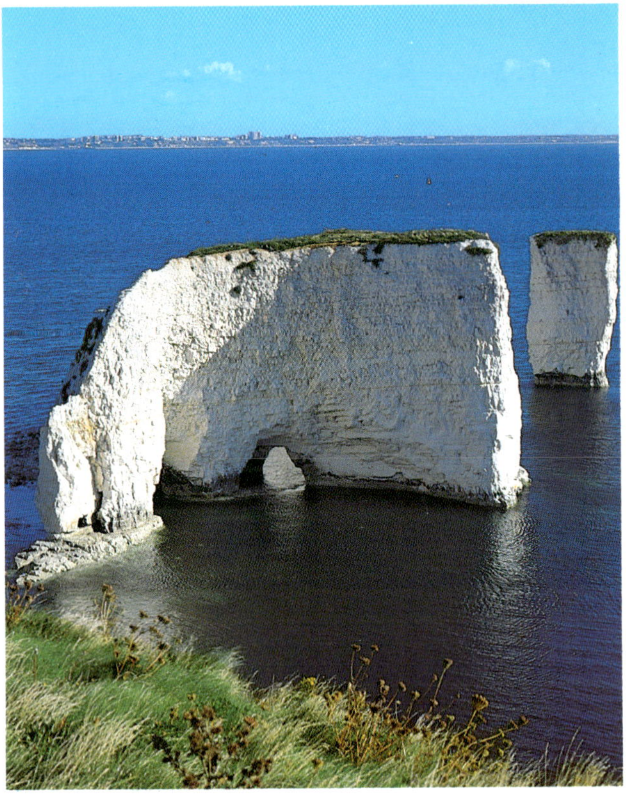

Old Harry Rocks

To the east of Corfe Castle a road leads out to **Studland**, a pretty, unspoiled village set in a secluded bay close to the sea, downs and woods. Many winding paths lead from the village to the excellent sandy beach which is owned by the National Trust. The wide bay at Studland affords a delightful view of the Isle of Wight and the Hampshire coast.

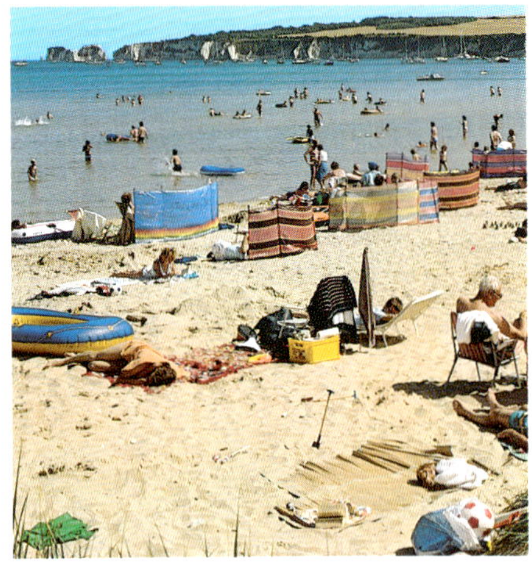

The Sands, Studland

Almost entirely land-locked, **Poole Harbour** is one of the largest natural harbours in the world. An ancient seaport and a modern resort, Poole attracts yachtsmen, fishermen and water-sports enthusiasts who benefit from the unusual double high tide which occurs on this stretch of the coast. A number of picturesque islands are dotted around the harbour, largest of which is Brownsea Island. Owned by the National Trust, it is both a bird sanctuary and a nature reserve, but is best known as the birthplace of the Scouting movement. It was here that Lord Baden-Powell hald the first Scout Camp in 1907.

Poole Harbour and Brownsea Island

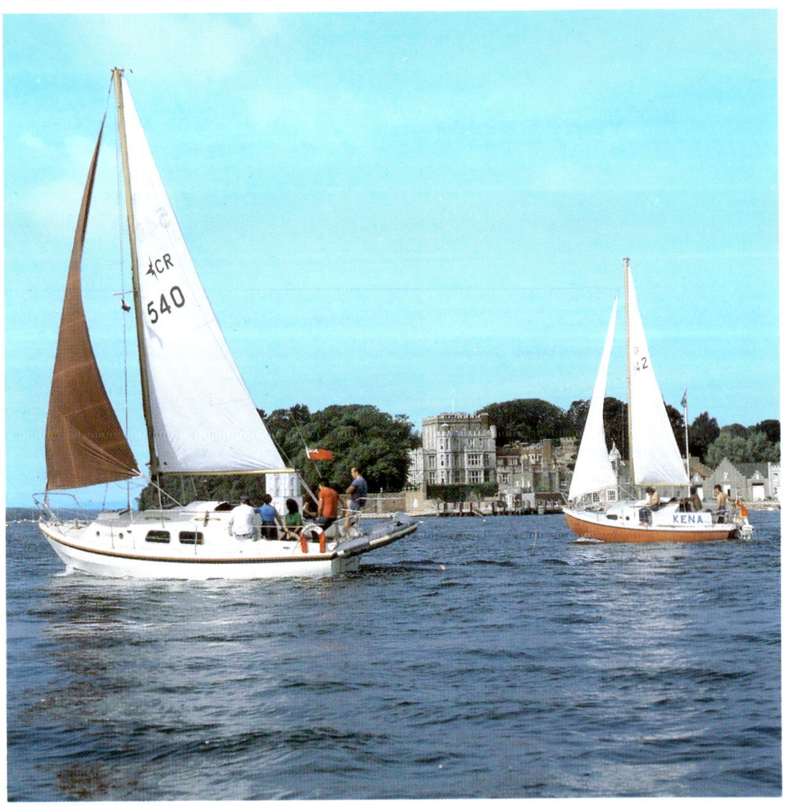

Superbly situated overlooking Poole Harbour, the beautiful ornamental gardens of **Compton Acres** were laid out soon after the First World War. Reputed to be some of the finest gardens in Europe, they contain many rare plants as well as some splendid marble and bronze statuary. The gardens, which also feature a Palm Court and fine woodland walks, are arranged in a variety of English and foreign styles. A number of them, including the delightful Italian Garden and the Japanese Garden, which was constructed by architects and workmen from Japan, include attractive water features.

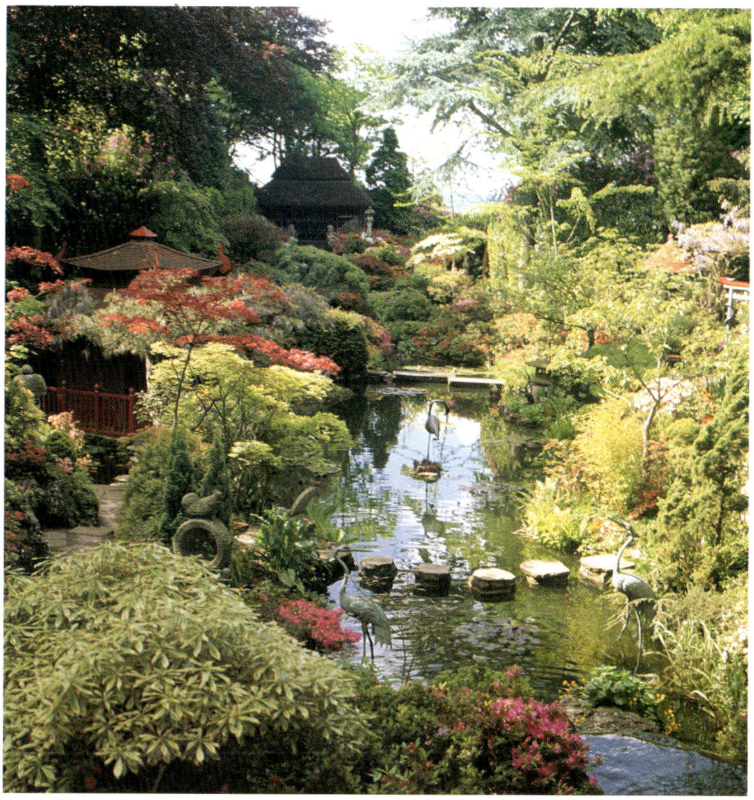

The Japanese Garden

The Italian Garden

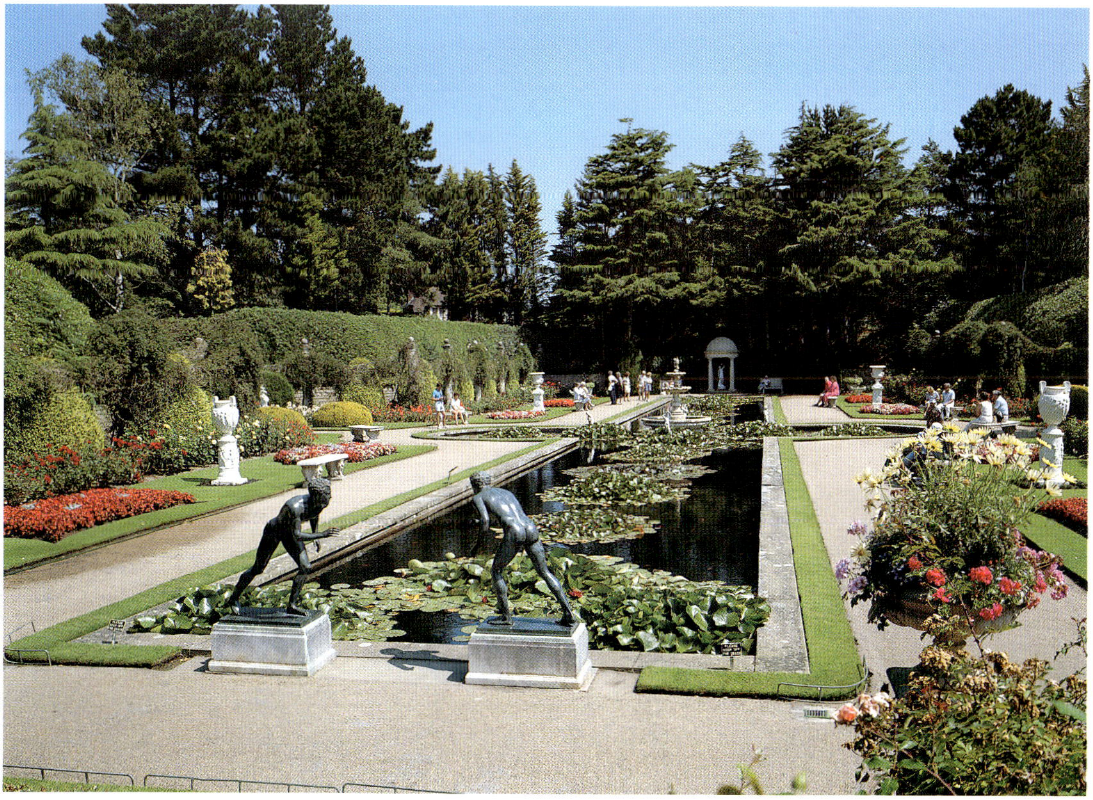

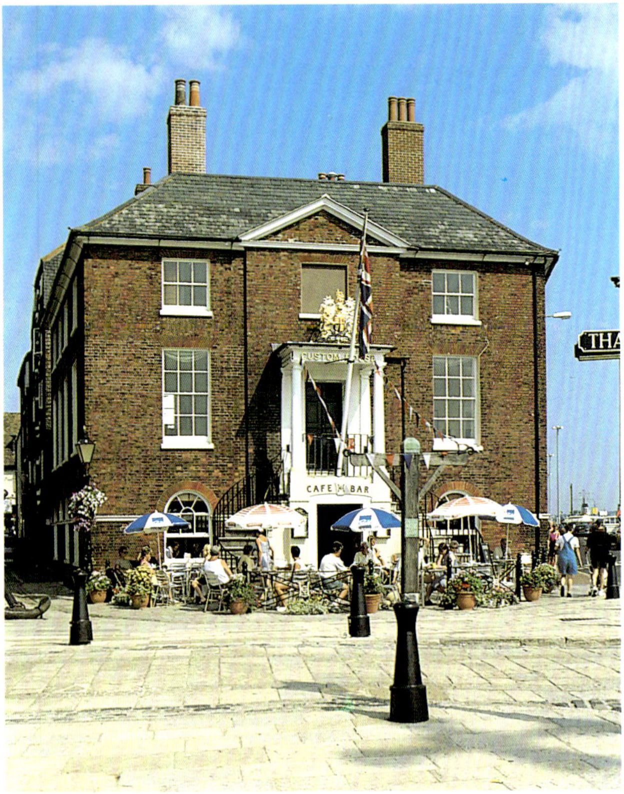

The Customs House

The older parts of **Poole** are to be found near the quayside, testifying to the importance of the town as a port from the earliest tmes. The lively waterfront of Poole Quay still bustles with small craft. the fine old Customs House, with its distinctive double flight of steps, stands on the quay near the Maritime Museum which celebrates Poole's seafaring traditions.

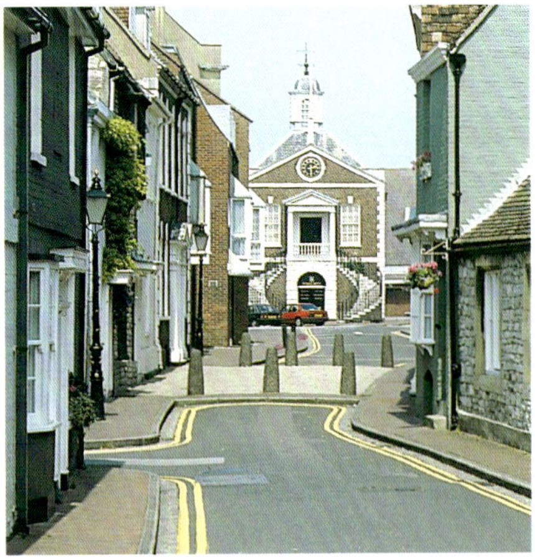

The Guildhall from Church Street

Bournemouth is a delightful garden city built among pines on the rim of a wide sandy bay. The beauty of the town is enhanced by picturesque chines or fissures in the cliff, rich with foliage, and also by many magnificent public parks and gardens. The Winter Gardens have been a well-known centre of entertainment for more than 100 years and the Lower, Central and Upper Gardens together extend for nearly two miles along the valley of the charming River Bourne. Central Gardens provide a secluded area shaded by fine trees.

Central Gardens, Bournemouth

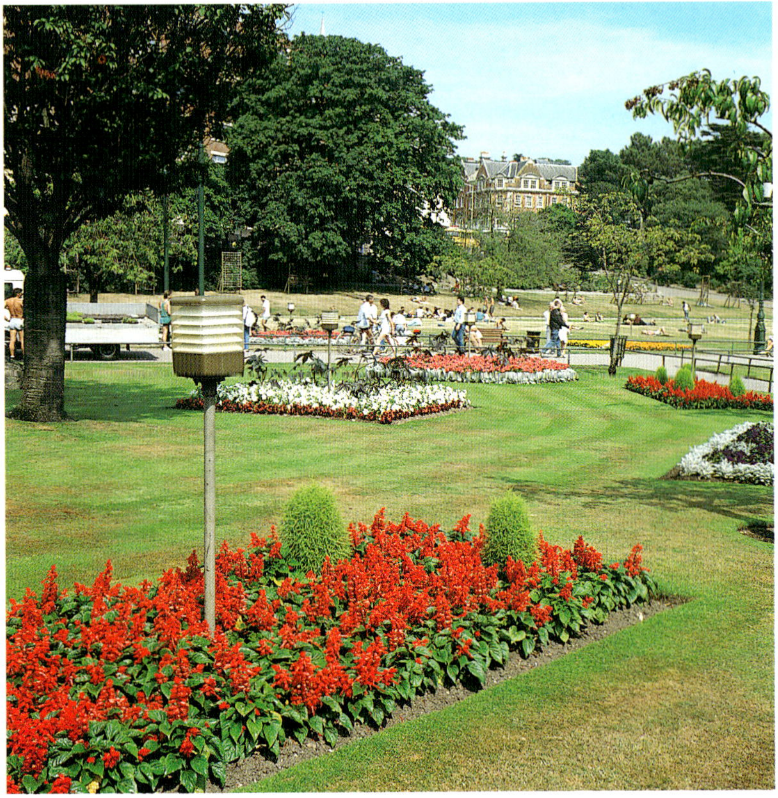

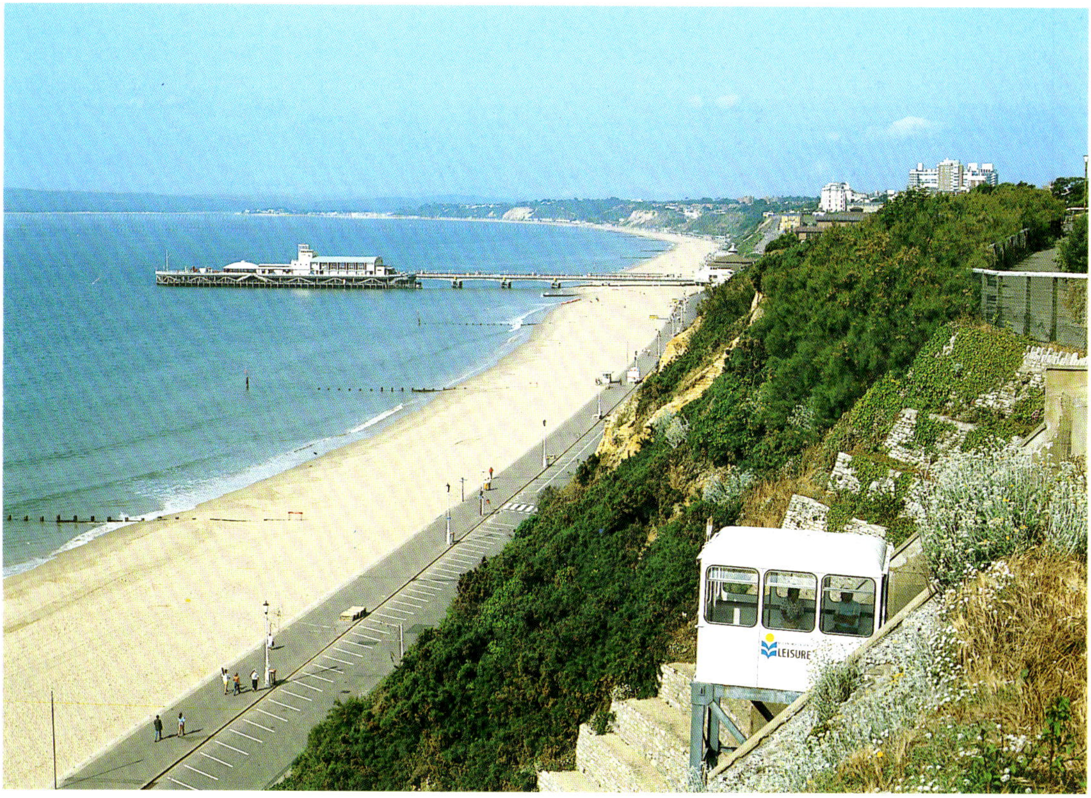

East Cliff Lift, Bournemouth

The International Centre and West Beach, Bournemouth

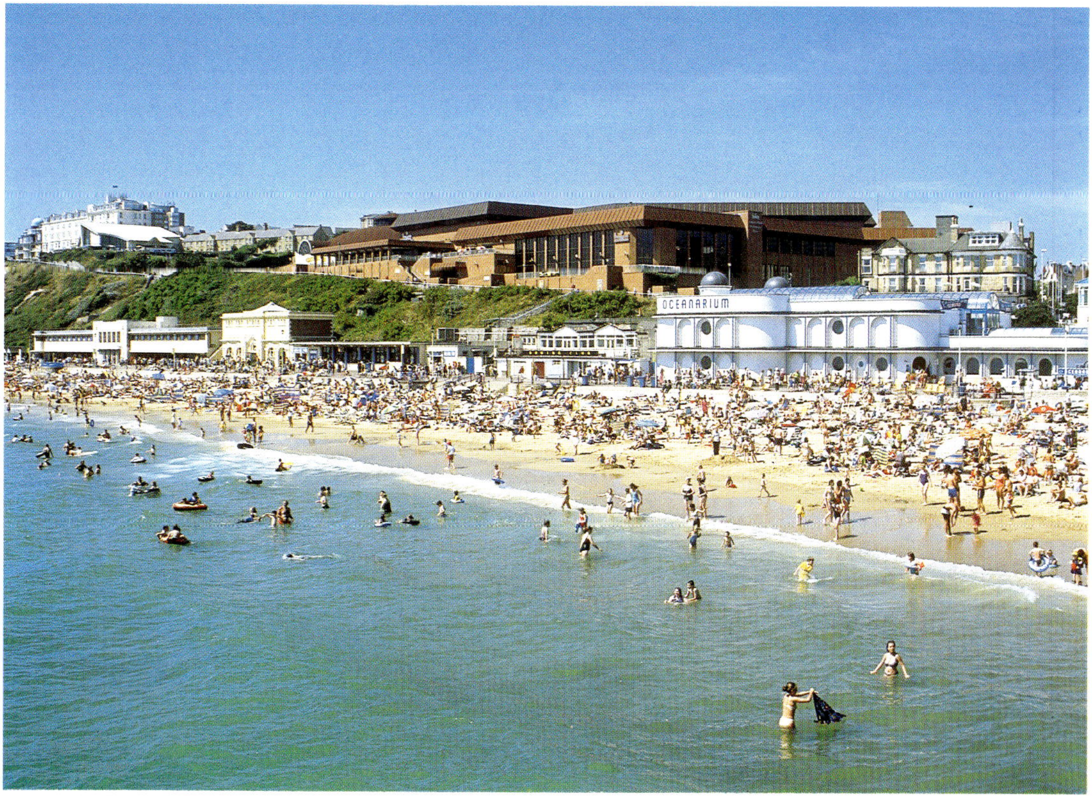

It was in the 18th century that **Bournemouth** was first developed as one of Britain's finest south coast resorts. Together with neighbouring Boscombe, it offers seven miles of sandy beaches. As a modern holiday centre Bournemouth is second to none with entertainment facilities which include the famous Pavilion, a pier with a theatre and the large International Centre. Situated on a magnificent bay, facing the English Channel, Bournemouth is ideally placed for visiting both the rugged Dorset coast and the peaceful glades of the New Forest.

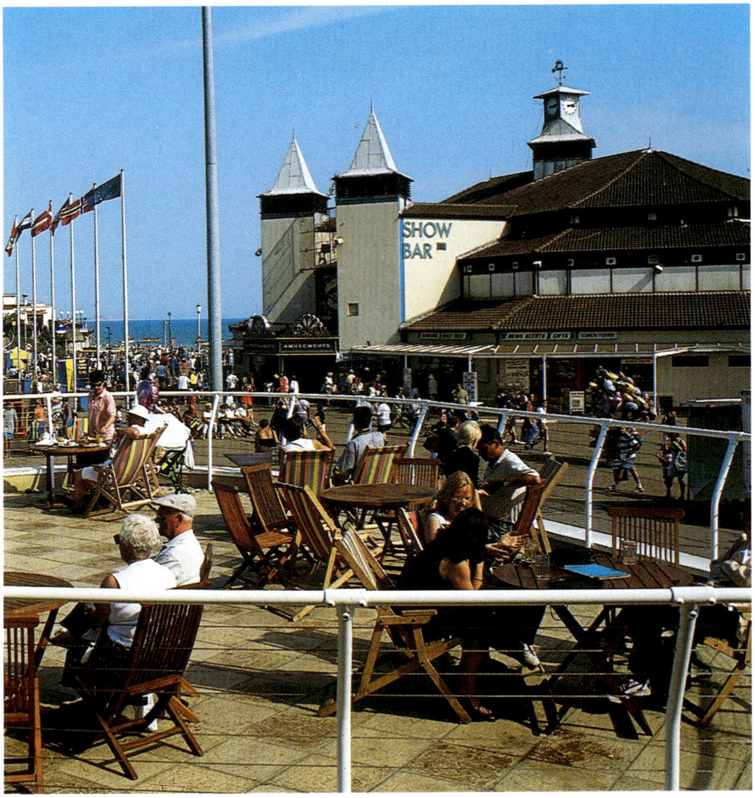

The Pier Approach, Bournemouth

The Sands, Boscombe

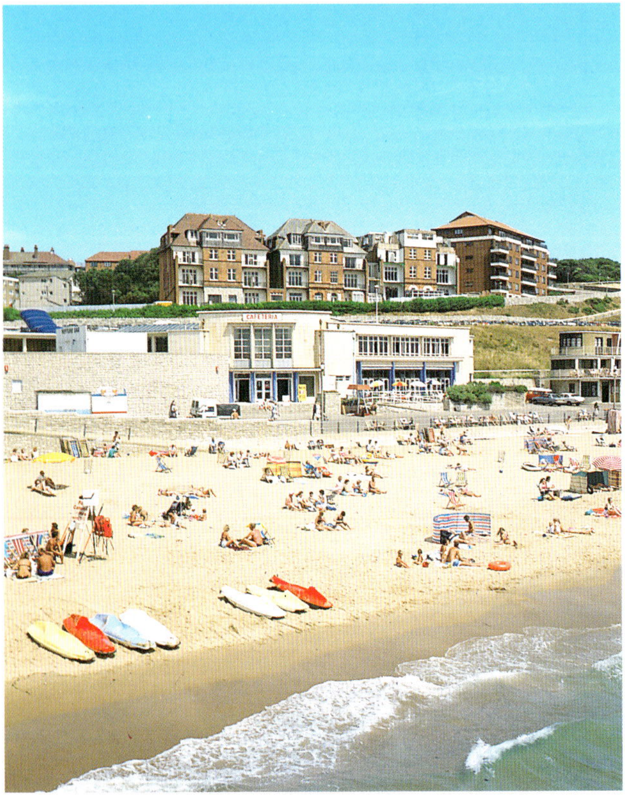

Situated east of Bournemouth on the sandy coast road which leads to Hengistbury Head, the popular holiday centre of **Boscombe** is in no way overshadowed by its larger neighbour. It has fine sands, its own pier offering traditional seaside amusements, a promenade and some attractive gardens.

Boscombe Chine

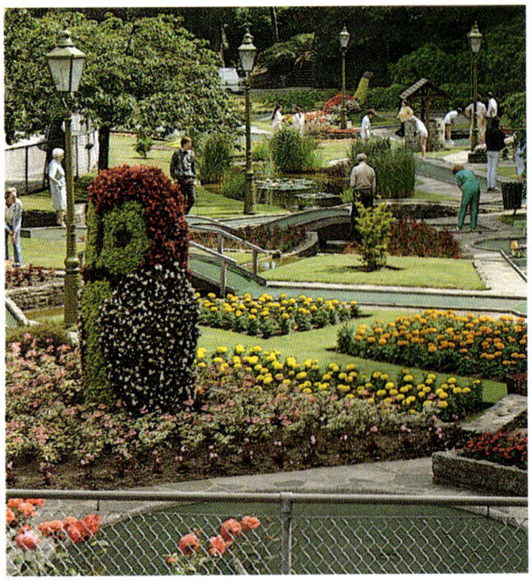

Christchurch, situated between the estuaries of the Rivers Stour and Avon, was originally a walled Saxon town. It was one of Alfred the Great's strongholds and the Saxon street plan can still be seen in the layout of the town centre. The ruins of a Norman castle, together with its constable's house, stand on the banks of the River Avon where the quayside is an attractive feature of the town. Boats can also be hired from the quay. The magnificent Priory Church was begun towards the end of the 11th century. It contains some notable Norman architecture including a superb turret on the north transept. At just over 300 feet, it is Britain's longest parish church and the tower holds two of the country's oldest bells which were both cast in 1370.

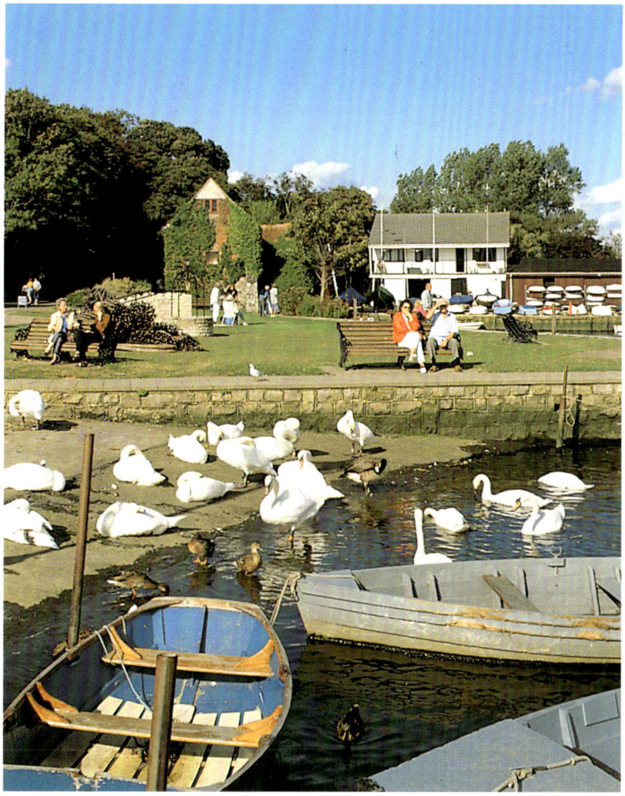

Town Quay, Christchurch

Christchurch Priory

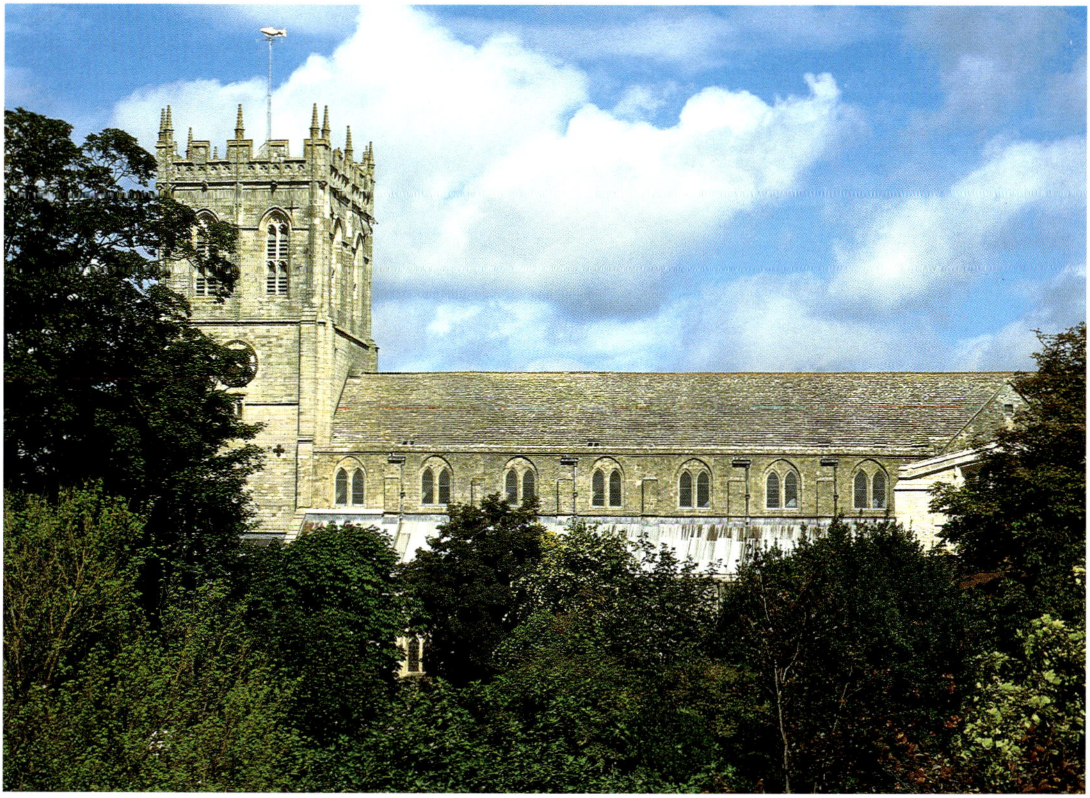

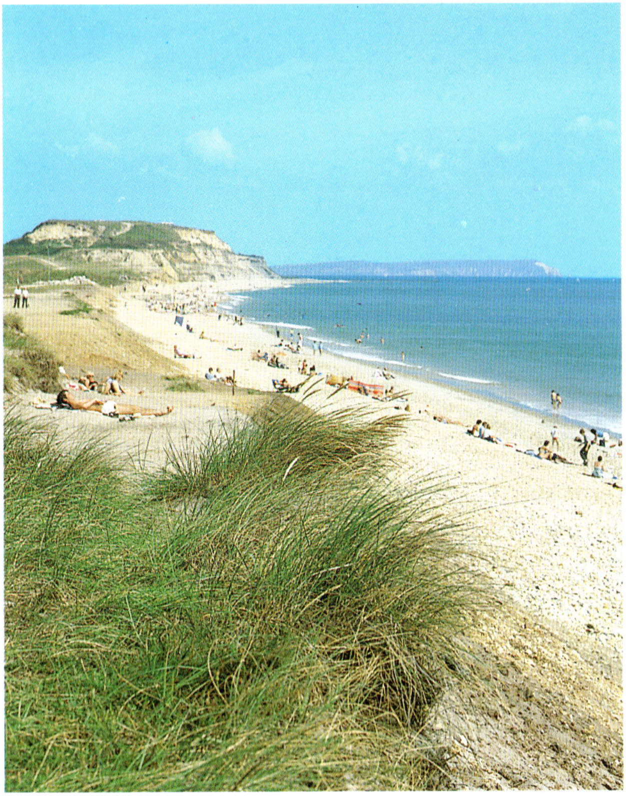

Hengistbury Head, Southbourne

Christchurch Harbour is an extensive area of shallow water sheltered by the two mile long spit of land known as **Hengistbury Head**. At the mouth of the harbour there is a narrow channel through which the tide ebbs and flows strongly but the harbour provides safe moorings and is therefore very popular with sailing enthusiasts. It has the unusual advantage of a double high tide which makes sailing and boating possible most of the time. Between Hengistbury Head and the popular resort of Bournemouth to the west, is **Southbourne**. Here a sheltered sandy beach is backed by marram grass and sand dunes. On the eastern tip of Christchurch Harbour opposite Hengistbury Head is the tiny village of **Mudeford** where lobster pots are often piled up on the quay. From here a ferry plies across the fast-flowing Avon Run.

The Run and the Quay, Mudeford

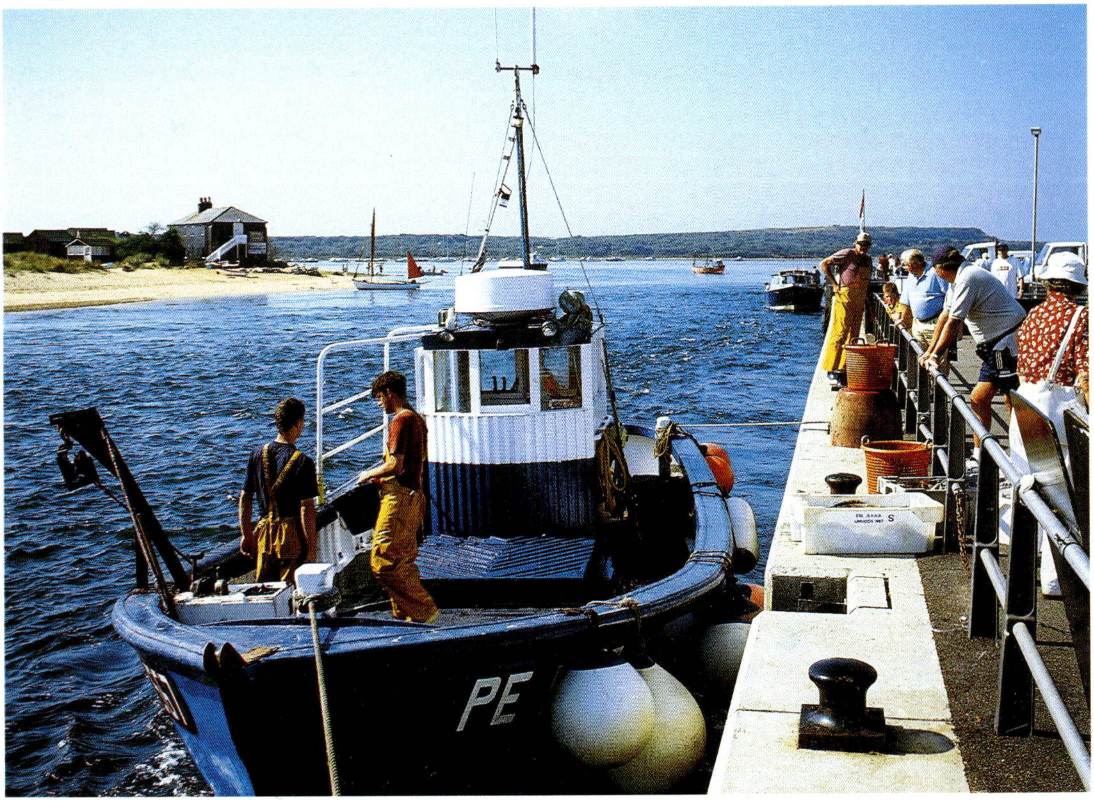

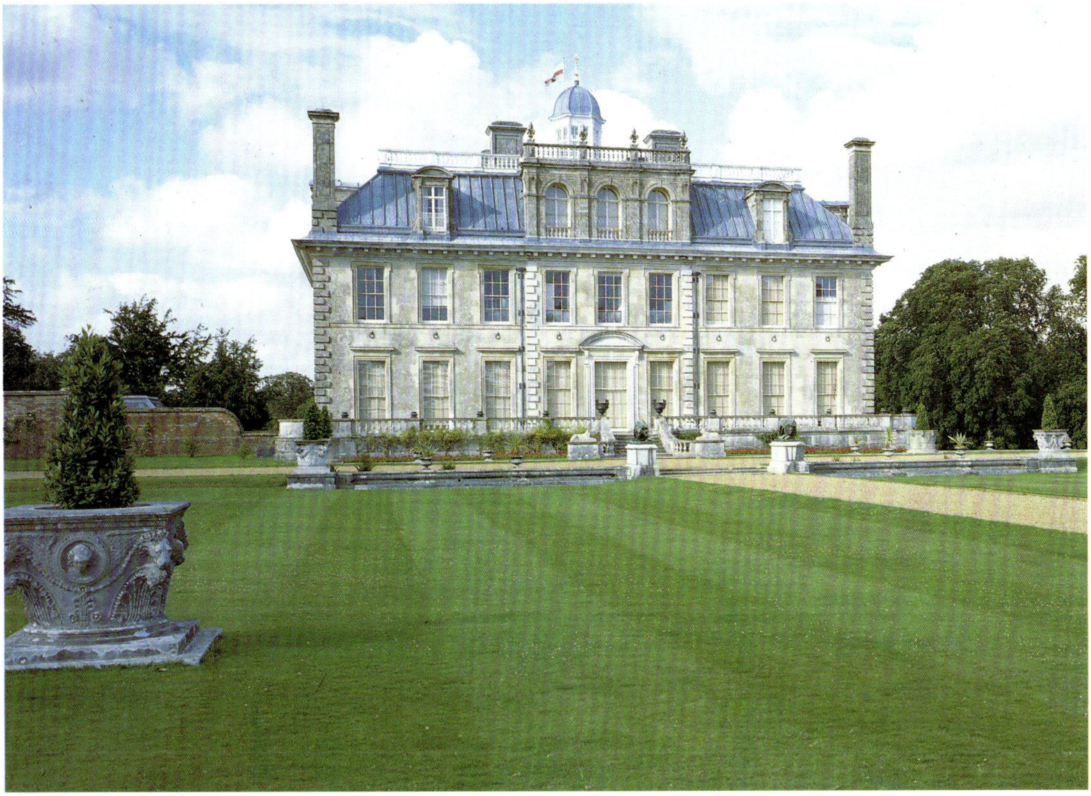

Kingston Lacy

The market town of **Wimborne Minster** stands on the River Stour which is crossed here by an ancient bridge, built in 1636 and reconstructed in the 19th century. At the heart of the town is the twin towered Minster Church, which exhibits many architectural styles from Norman to late Gothic. One of the church's unusual features is a 14th century clock. The figure of a grenadier holding a hammer in each hand with which to strike the quarter-hours was immortalised in a poem by Thomas Hardy who lived for a time in Wimborne Minster. Built during the 1660s, **Kingston Lacy** is a magnificent country house standing in extensive grounds. It was considerably altered in the 19th century by Sir Charles Barry, the designer of the Houses of Parliament.

Wimborne Minster

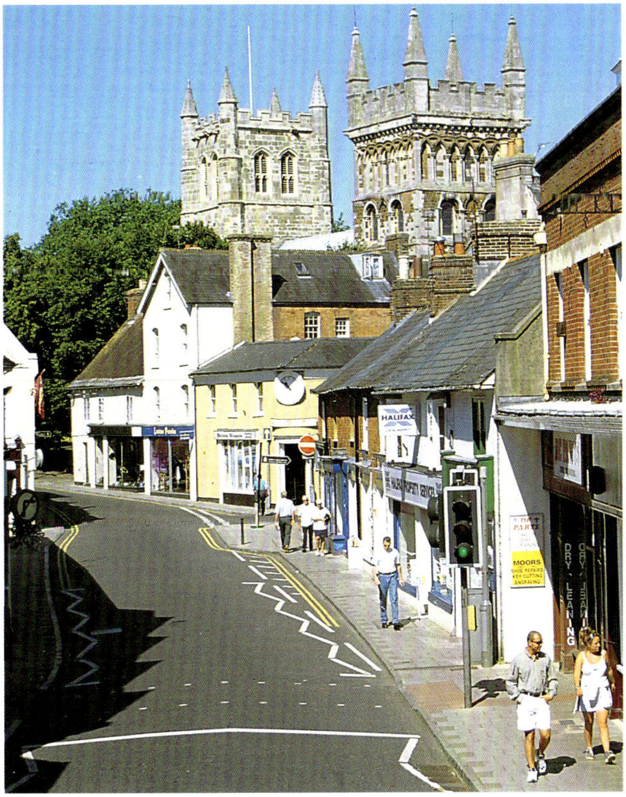

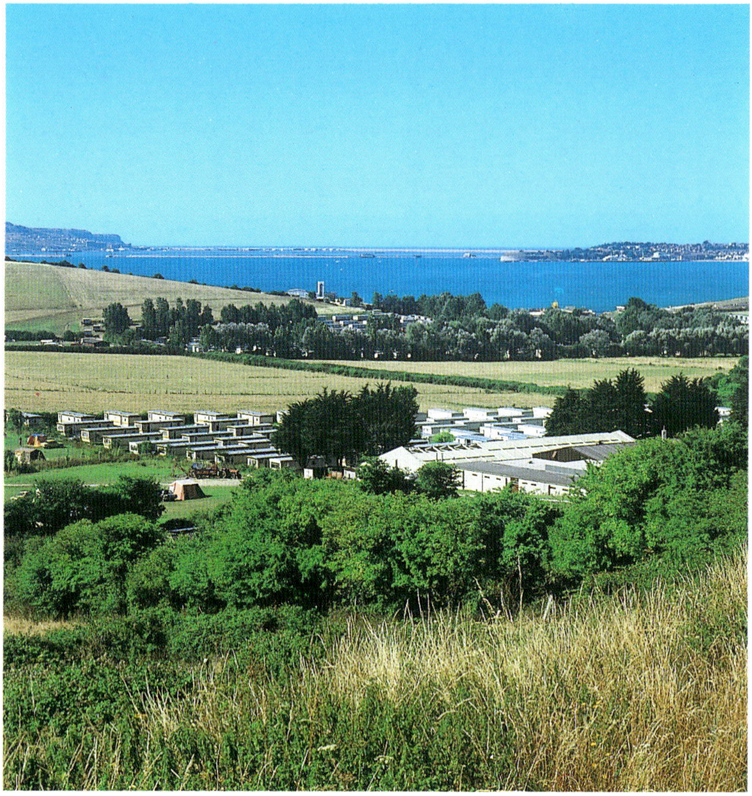

The glorious curve of **Weymouth Bay** is one of the finest on the south coast. Sheltered by the peninsula of the Isle of Portland, it is nearly five miles across and about two and a half miles from north to south. At the north end of the bay attractive **Bowleaze Cove** has a beach of sand, shingle and rock-pools and above the cove Furzy Cliff, a popular spot for picnics, overlooks the sweep of the bay. A cliff-top path connects Bowleaze to Osmington Mills with its 13th century Smugglers Inn and nearby is the charming inland village of **Osmington** with its picturesque cottages.

Weymouth Bay

Of the many white horses which are found in southern England, the huge equestrian figure of George III at **Osmington** is amongst the most widely known. Cut into the chalk hillside, it was created in 1808 and is 280 feet long by 323 feet high.

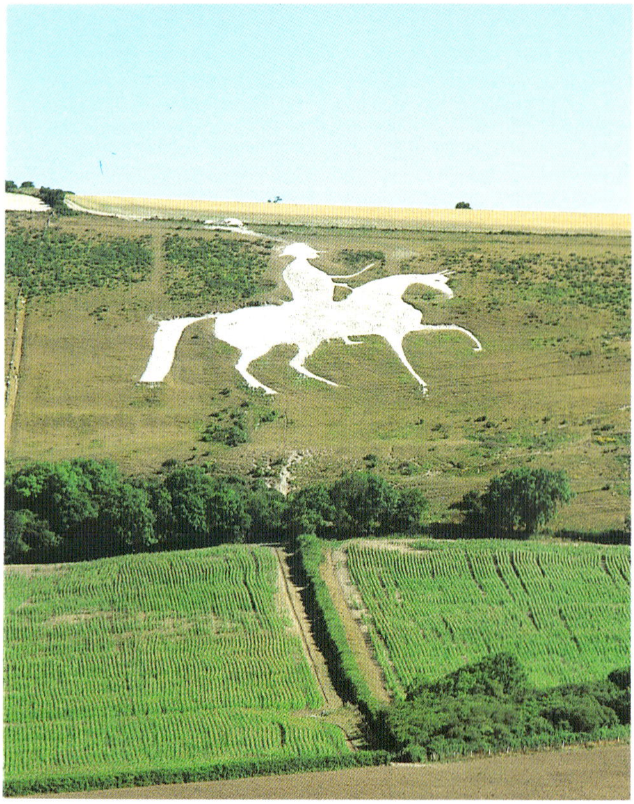

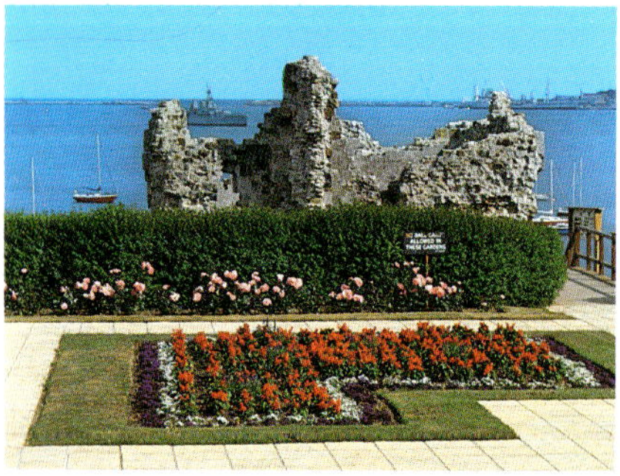

To the south of the resort of Weymouth stand the remains of **Sandsfoot Castle**, one of a chain of coastal forts built by Henry VIII. Maintained as a harbour defence until about 1700, the ruins are surrounded by attractive gardens.

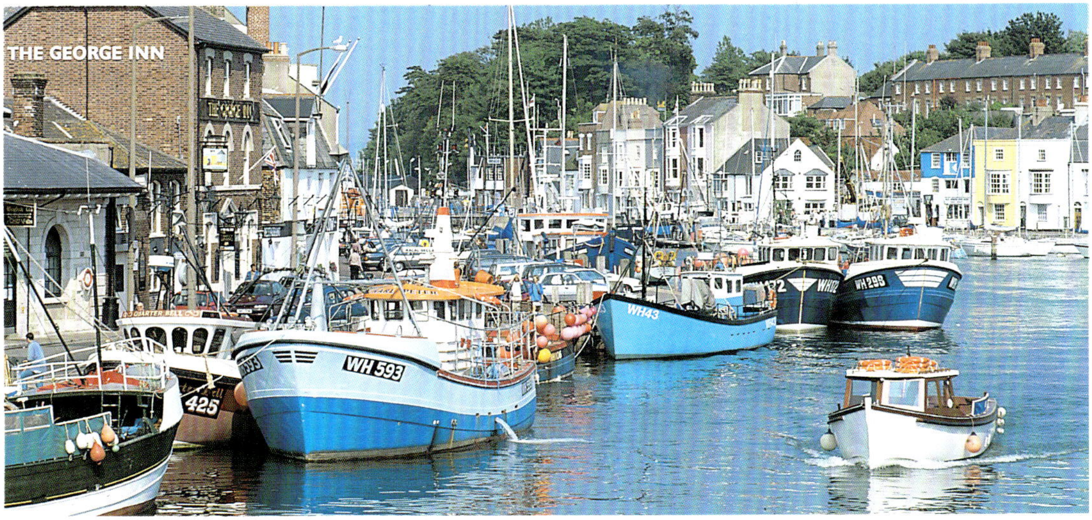

The Harbour

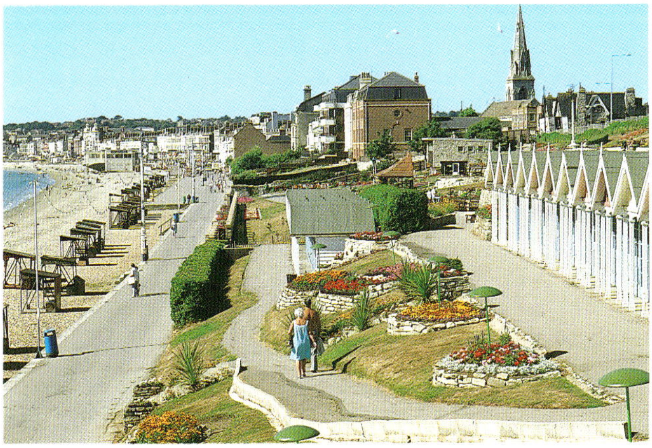

Greenhill Gardens

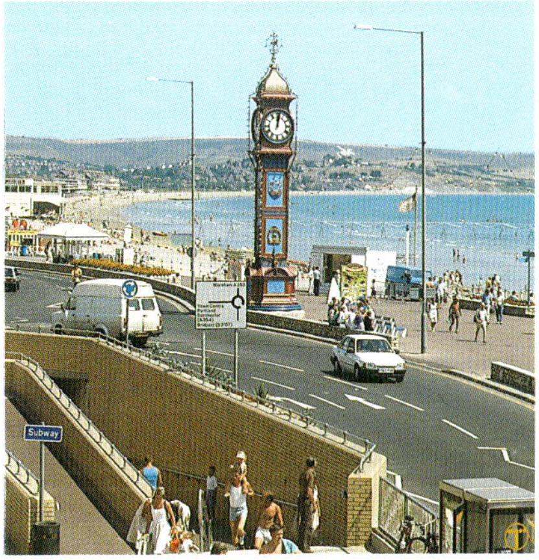

The Clock Tower

Weymouth's popularity as a resort was ensured when George III visited the town in 1789 and was the first reigning monarch to make use of a bathing machine. A wide esplanade fronts many pleasant Georgian buildings and follows the curve of the bay past the elaborate clock tower, erected in 1887 to mark Queen Victoria's golden jubilee. At the northern end of the esplanade, Greenhill Gardens provide a peaceful retreat and have lovely views across the sandy beach to the sea. Weymouth was originally a seaport and in its busy harbour, at the mouth of the River Wey, fishing boats and pleasure craft still mingle.

The Beach

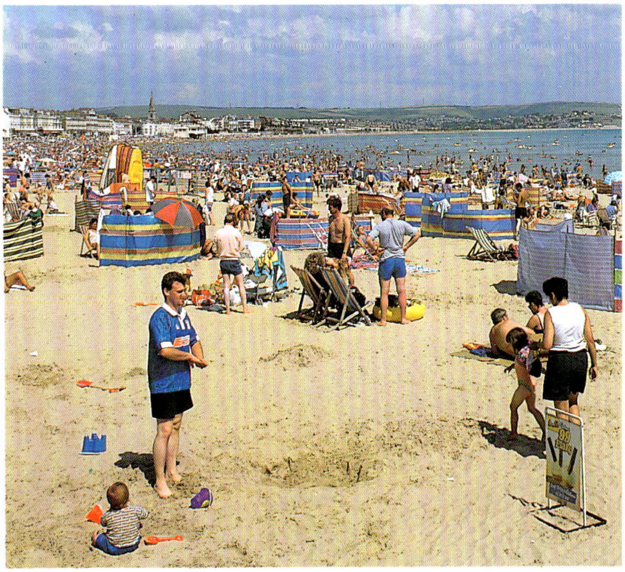

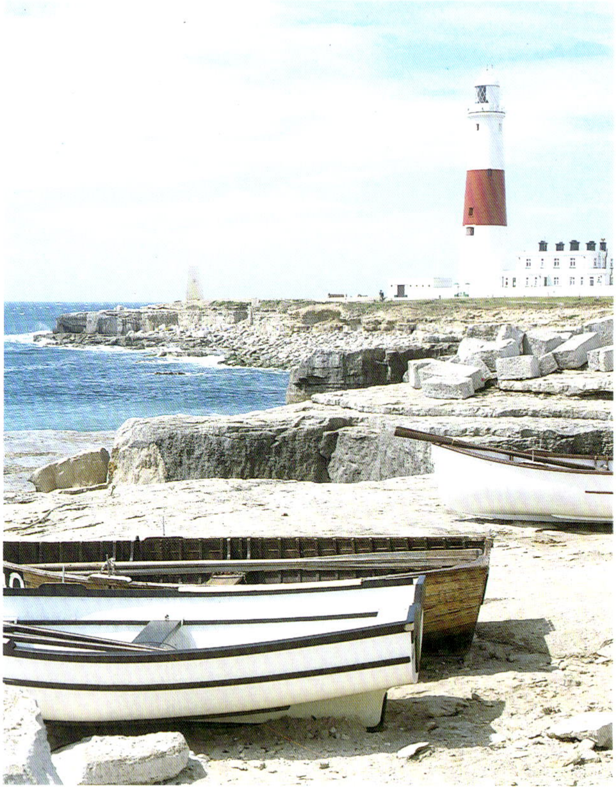

Portland Lighthouse and Bill

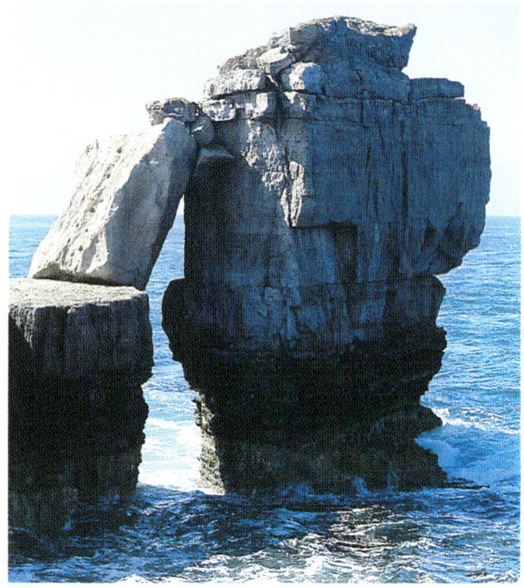

Pulpit Rock

Connected to the mainland by a narrow neck of land, the limestone peninsula of Portland culminates at **Portland Bill.** Here stands the 136 feet high lighthouse which was built in 1903-06 to replace two earlier structures and nearby is the huge, detached block of stone known as **Pulpit Rock.**

Chesil from Portland

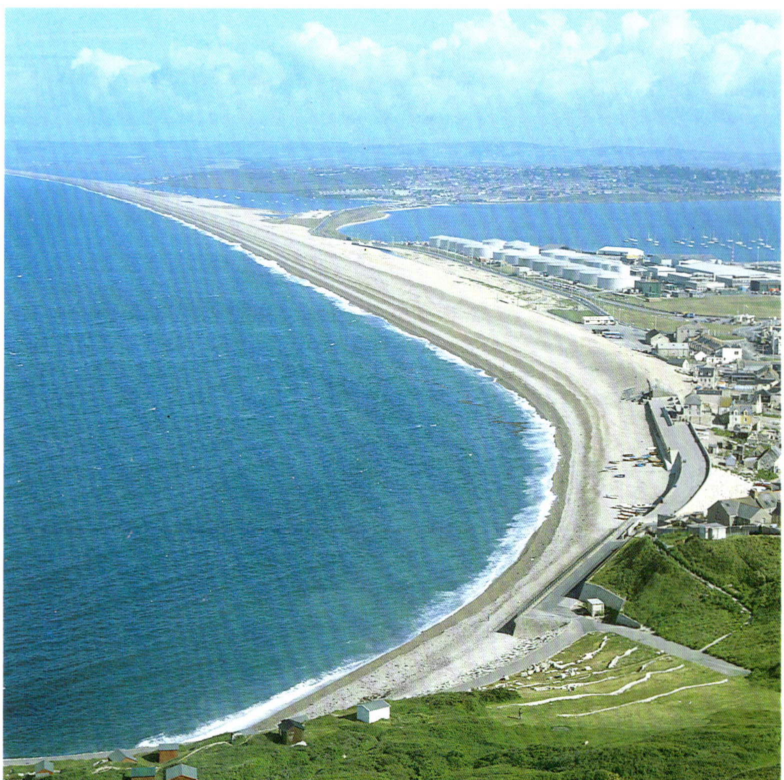

Running north-west from Portland along Lyme Bay is the unique **Chesil Bank**. Formed over many thousands of years, this great pebble ridge extends almost to West Bay and separates the Fleet, a ten mile long backwater, from the sea. It is forty feet high in places and has been the graveyard of many fine sailing ships. Geologists have been unable to decide how the pebbles come to be graded for size. They range from less than one inch in diameter in the west to in excess of three and a half inches at Portland.

Abbotsbury, which is situated in a valley of outstanding natural beauty, is an ancient village of thatched, stone-built houses. It is famous for its Swannery which lies on a long strip of water known as the Fleet at the western end of Chesil Beach overlooking Lyme Bay. This is the only nesting colony of mute swans in Britain and in winter the resident number of birds doubles to nearly one thousand. The Swannery dates from the 11th century when Benedictine monks reared the birds for meat. It was also the monks who built Abbotsbury's fine 15th century tithe barn. At 272 feet long it is one of the largest and finest tithe barns in the country. Formerly a granary, it once contained a water mill within its walls but now it houses a country museum.

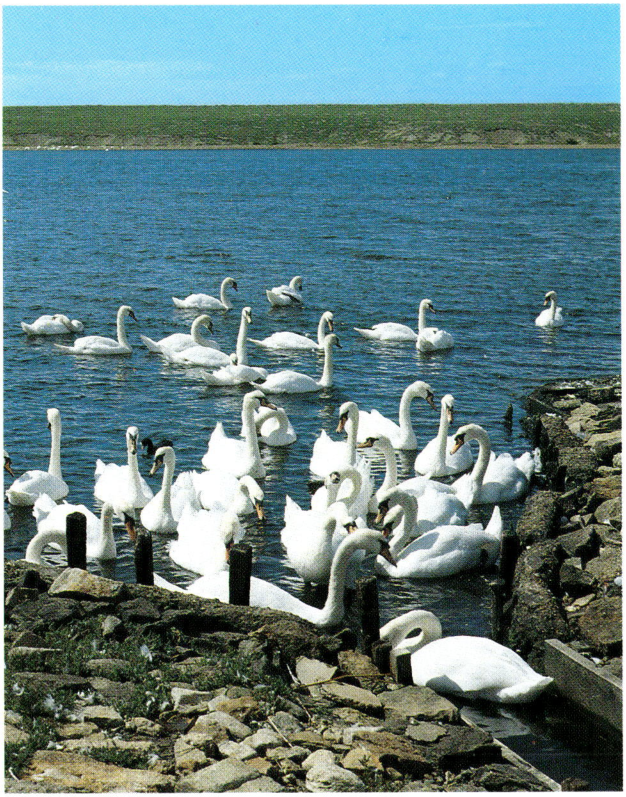

The Swannery

The Tithe Barn

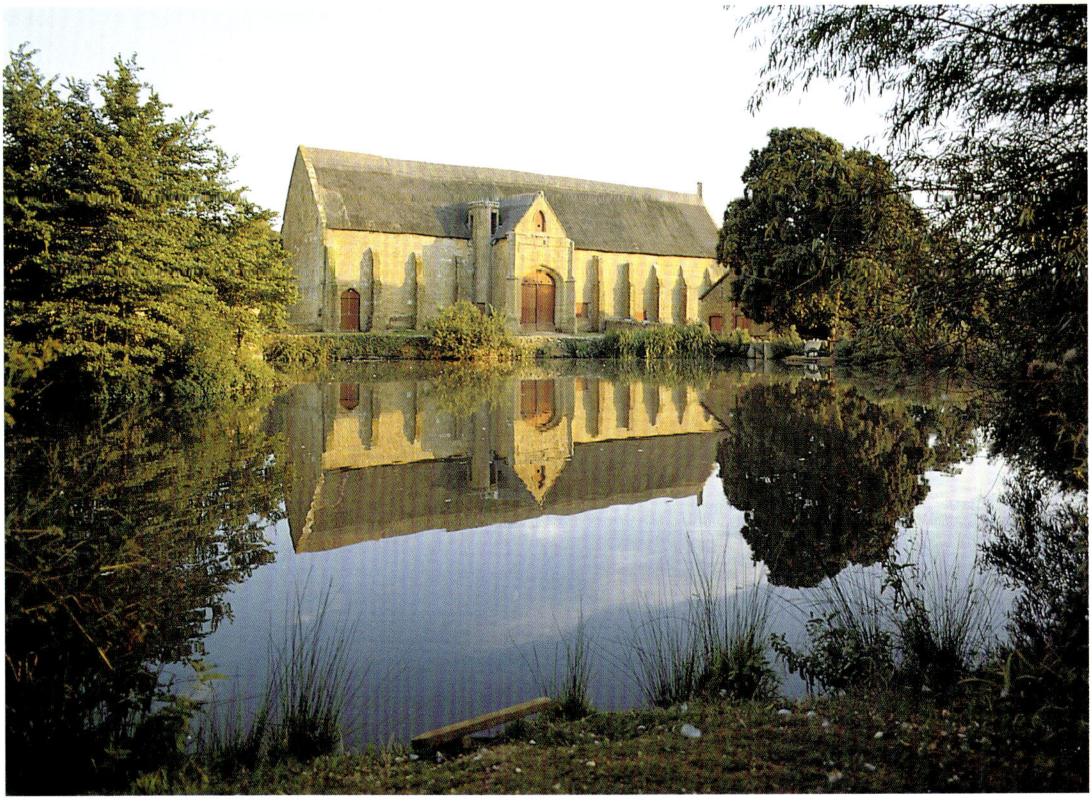

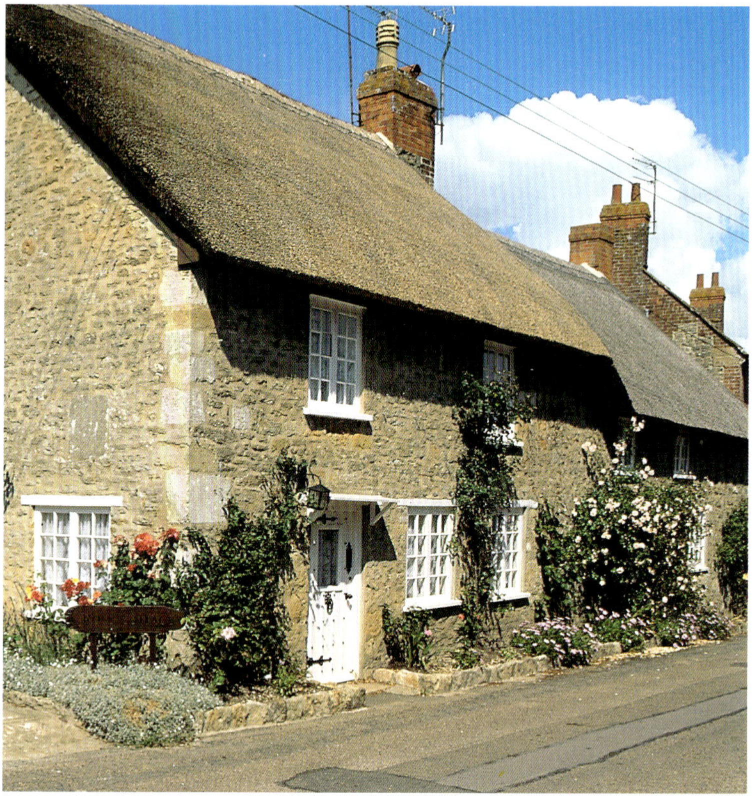

Cottages at Burton Bradstock

Burton Bradstock lies on the coast between Abbotsbury and Bridport and is a delightfully unspoilt example of a rural Dorset village. Its numerous lovely cottages are an immense attraction for visitors and artists from the nearby resorts. Many of them date from the 17th century and, as they crowd together in narrow, twisting lanes, their appearance has altered little since that time. Not far from the triangular village green, an interesting 14th century parish church stands beside the village school.

Less than a mile from the attractive village of Burton Bradstock, at the western end of Chesil Beach, is the popular **Freshwater Beach**. Here the River Bride reaches the sea and the beach is a favourite spot for bathing and picnics.

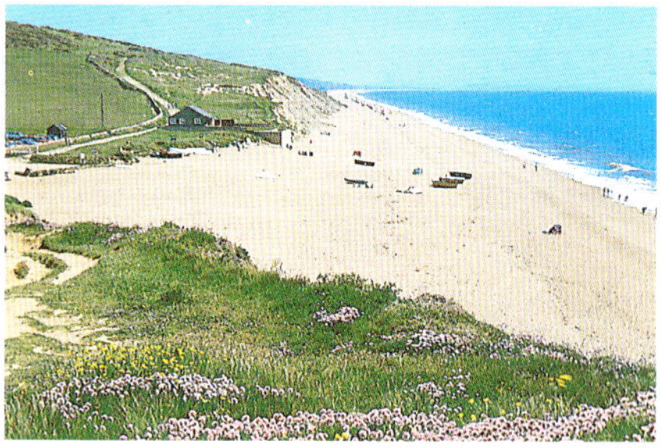

Chesil Beach, seen here from Burton Bradstock at its western extremity, takes its name from the Anglo-Saxon word "chesil" meaning shingle. This remarkable natural feature is rich in geological specimens and provides a home for a wide variety of birds, fishes and plants.

Freshwater Beach

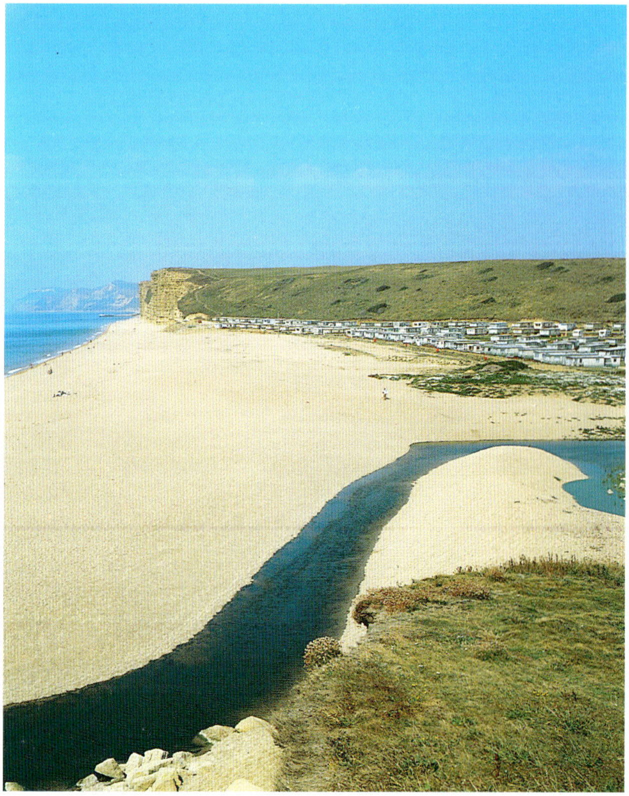

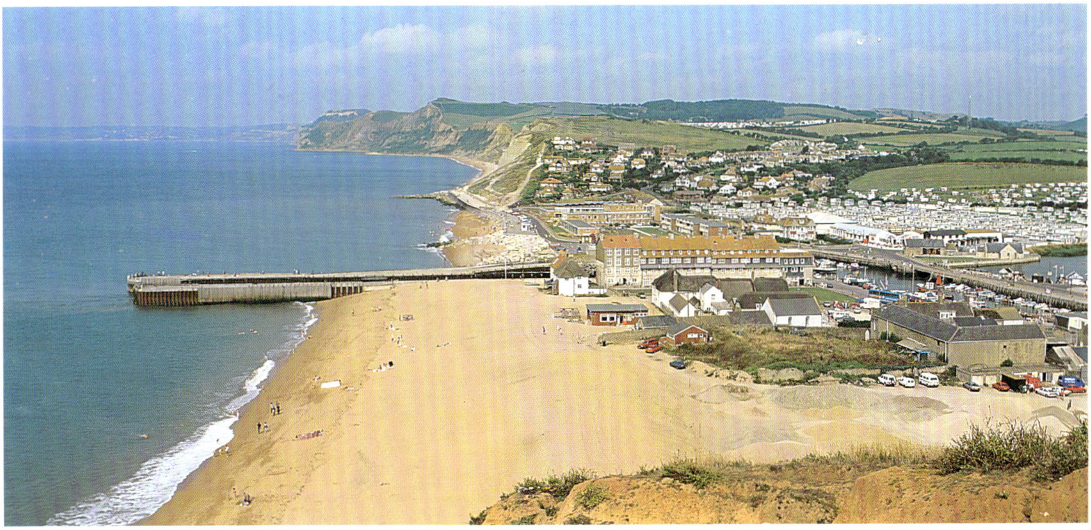

West Bay

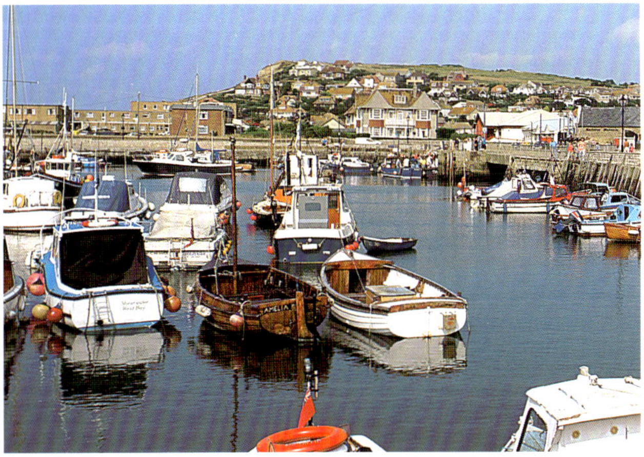

The Harbour, West Bay

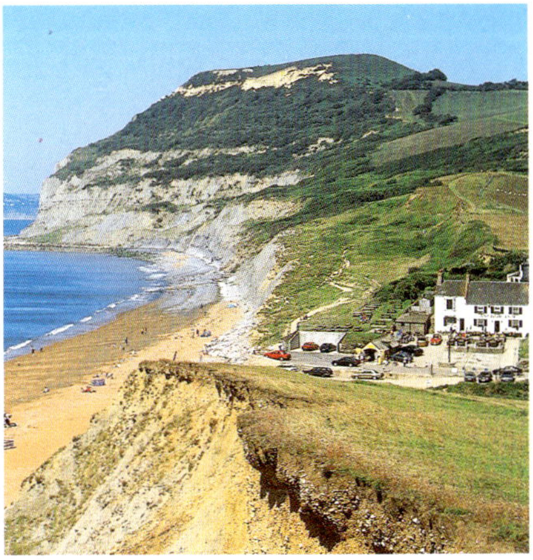

Seatown and Golden Cap

Town Hall, Bridport

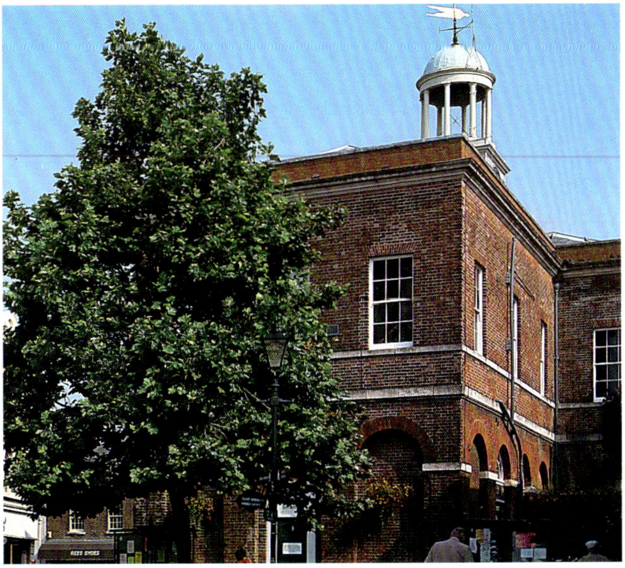

West Bay, facing the great sweep of Lyme Bay, was built as the harbour for Bridport, two miles inland. It has now become a seaside resort at the mouth of the River Brit and the great mass of East Cliff dominates the beach. **Bridport** itself is an ancient town, long associated with the production of rope and netting twines which were once laid out along the wide main streets. Lined with elegant Georgian houses, these streets converge on the arcaded 18th century Town Hall. About two miles to the west is **Seatown** where the golden shingle beach is dominated by the 626 feet high bulk of Golden Cap, the highest cliff in southern England.

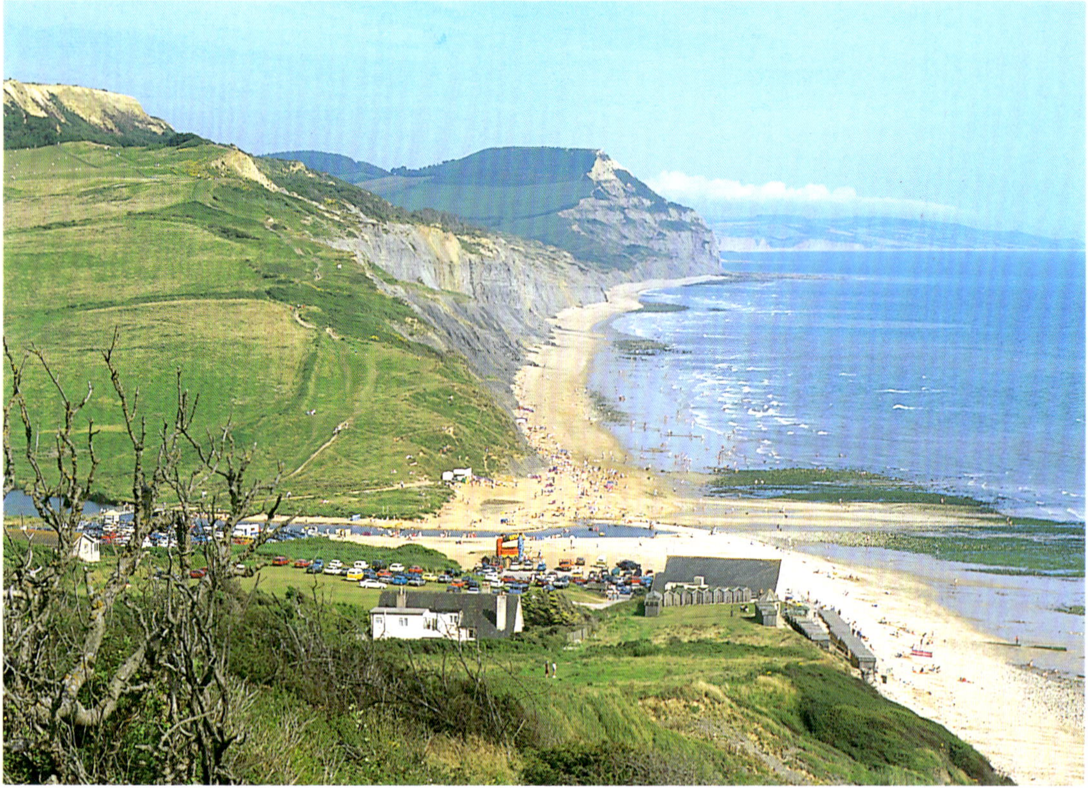

Charmouth from the Cliffs

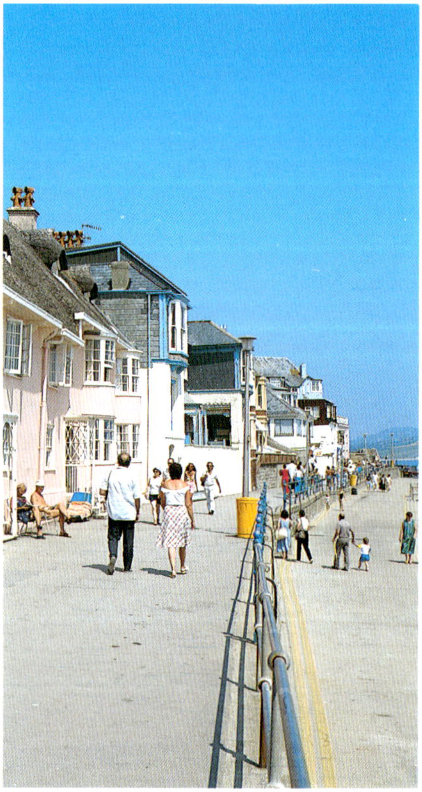

Marine Parade, Lyme Regis

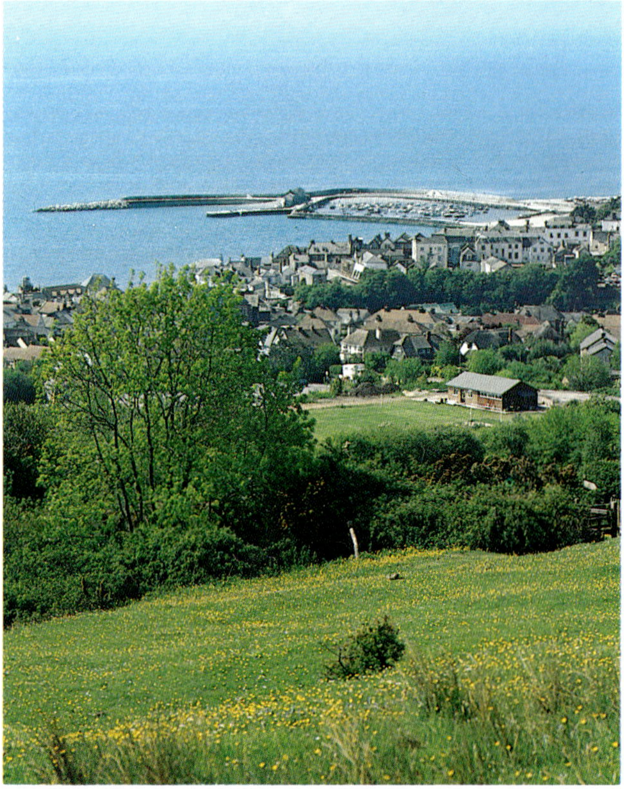

The Town and the Cobb

Charmouth is a popular summer resort with a fine stretch of pebble and sand beach. The village is set half-a-mile back from the shore and consists mainly of one long street lined with dignified Georgian houses, old thatched cottages and inns. **Lyme Regis** is a pleasant old town at the foot of two steep hills. It has a tiny promenade with some attractive Georgian cottages but perhaps its most interesting feature is the small harbour enclosed by a curving breakwater known as the Cobb. First built about 1300 AD by local fishermen, the harbour was the landing place of the ill-fated Duke of Monmouth in 1685 at the start 9of his abortive rebellion. Lyme Regis first achieved prosperity in medieval times, but it was in the mid-18th century that it became popular as a resort. Jane Austen visited the town in 1803 and based part of her novel *Persuasion* here.

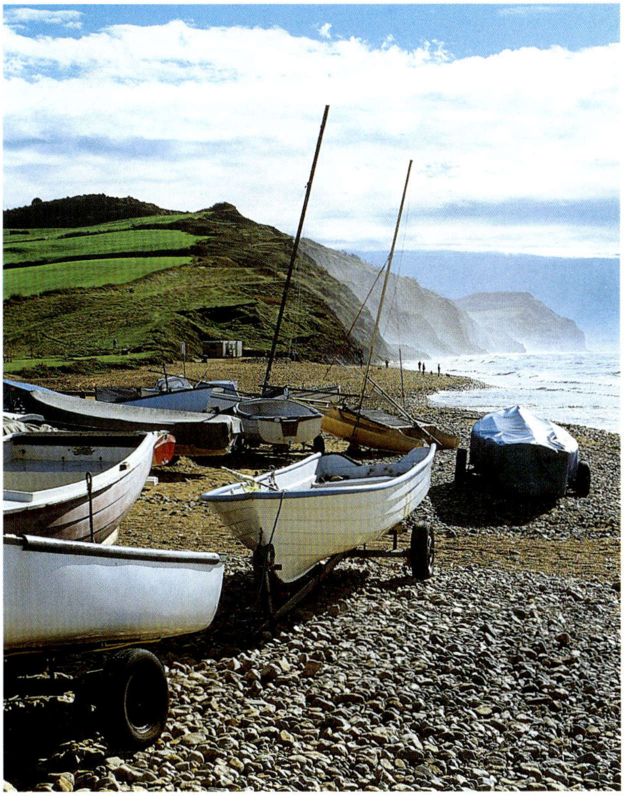

The Beach, Charmouth

Lyme Bay

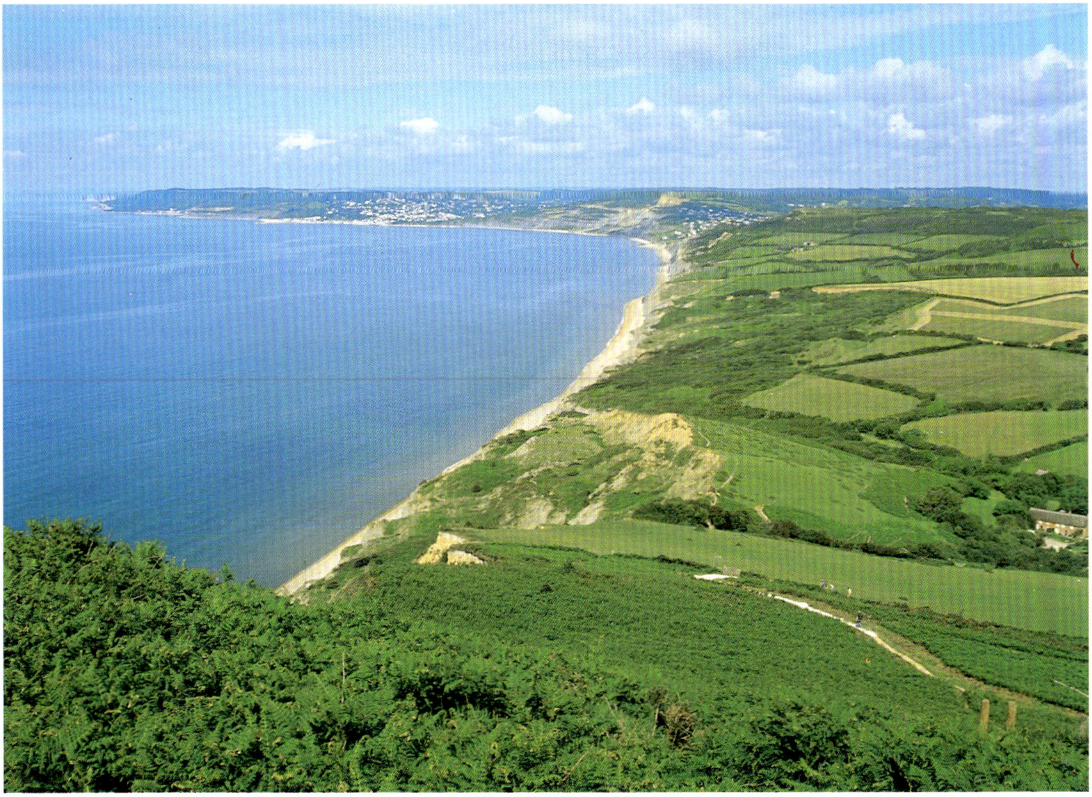

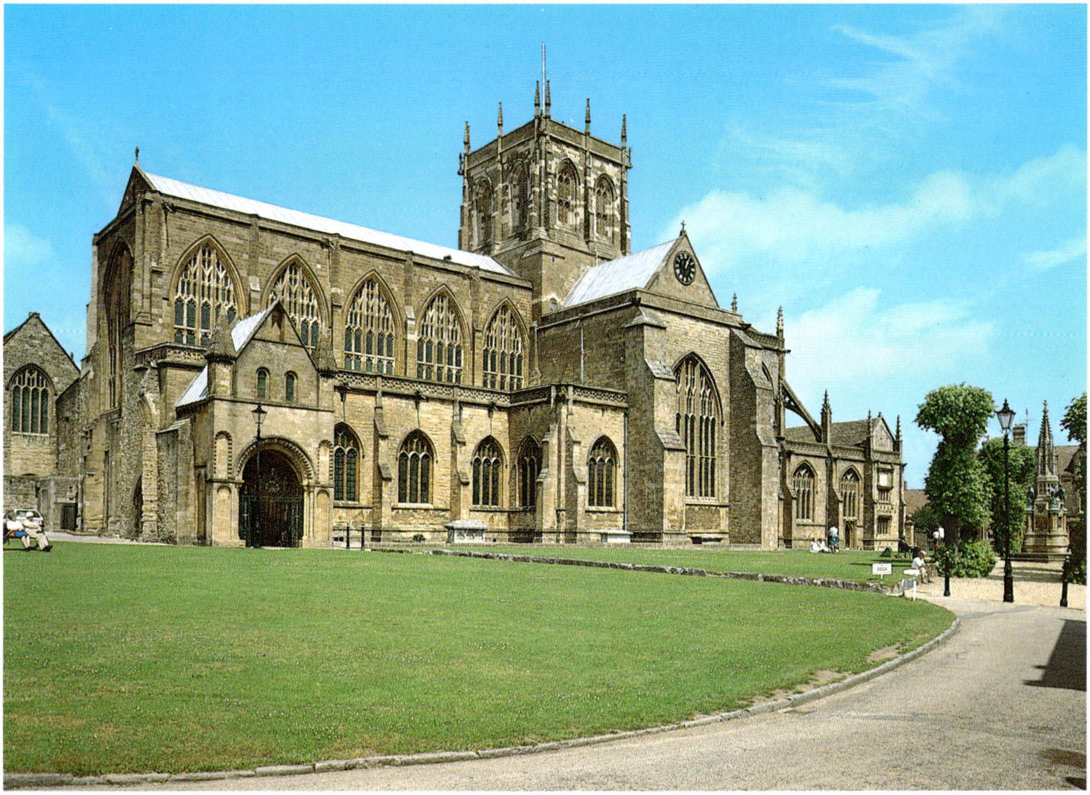

The Almshouses and Abbey, Sherborne

The Mill, Sturminster Newton

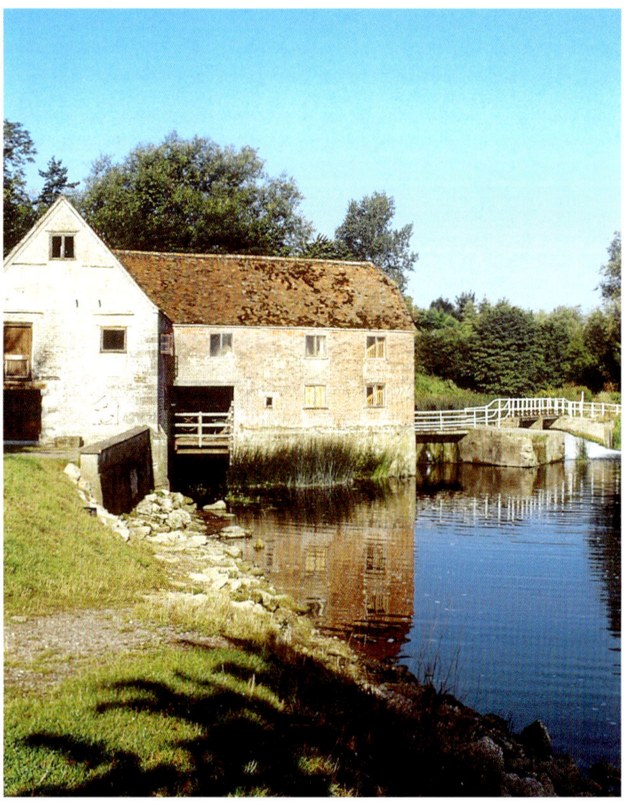

Ancient **Sherborne** is a town of warm stone buildings set amongst green hills on the River Yeo. Among its many interesting old buildings are the well-known Sherborne School and the Abbey Church which is especially noted for its fan-vaulting. The choir is said to be the finest example of Perpendicular work in existence. At the foot of Cheap Street stands a 14th century conduit which once stood within the abbey cloisters and was a wash house for the monks. Near the ancient market town of **Sturminster Newton** an old mill stands on the banks of the River Stour which is spanned here by a fine six-arched medieval bridge. This bears one of the famous Dorset Transportation Tablets, warning of the dire penalty which awaits anyone who causes "injury" to the bridge.

Shaftesbury is an ancient market town occupying a dramatic situation on a high spur of land. This commanding position led Alfred the Great to choose the site as one of the principal towns in his kingdom of Wessex. Today Shaftesbury is rich in historical remains and its most famous and picturesque landmark is Gold Hill. This ancient cobbled street, first recorded in 1362, affords magnificent views over Blackmore Vale. With its pretty tiled and thatched cottages, Gold Hill is a fascinating reminder of the town's hisory. **Blandford Forum** has also been an important market town from early times but was largely destroyed by fire in 1731. The rebuilt town is an outstanding example of Georgian architecture and the Church of St. Peter and St. Paul, designed by the same architects who planned the elegant town centre, is one of the finest churches of the period.

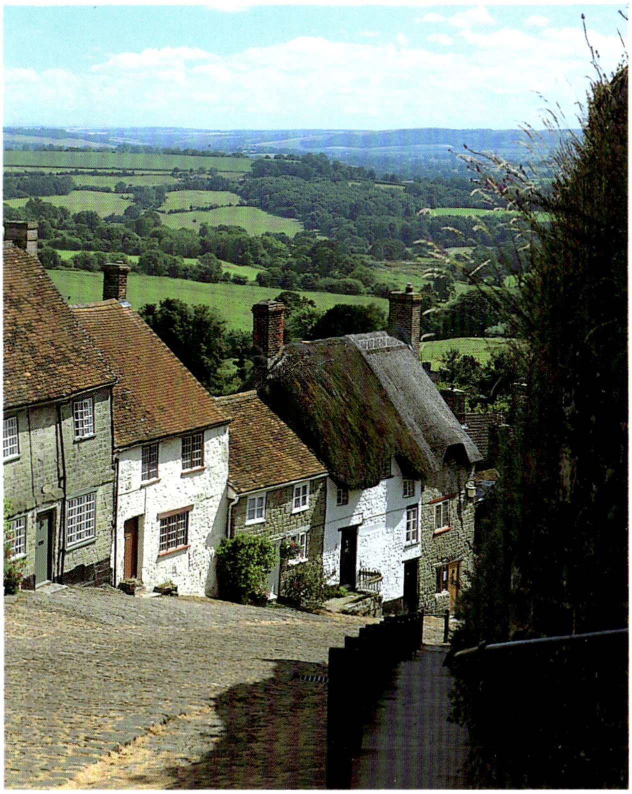

Gold Hill

The Market Place, Blandford Forum

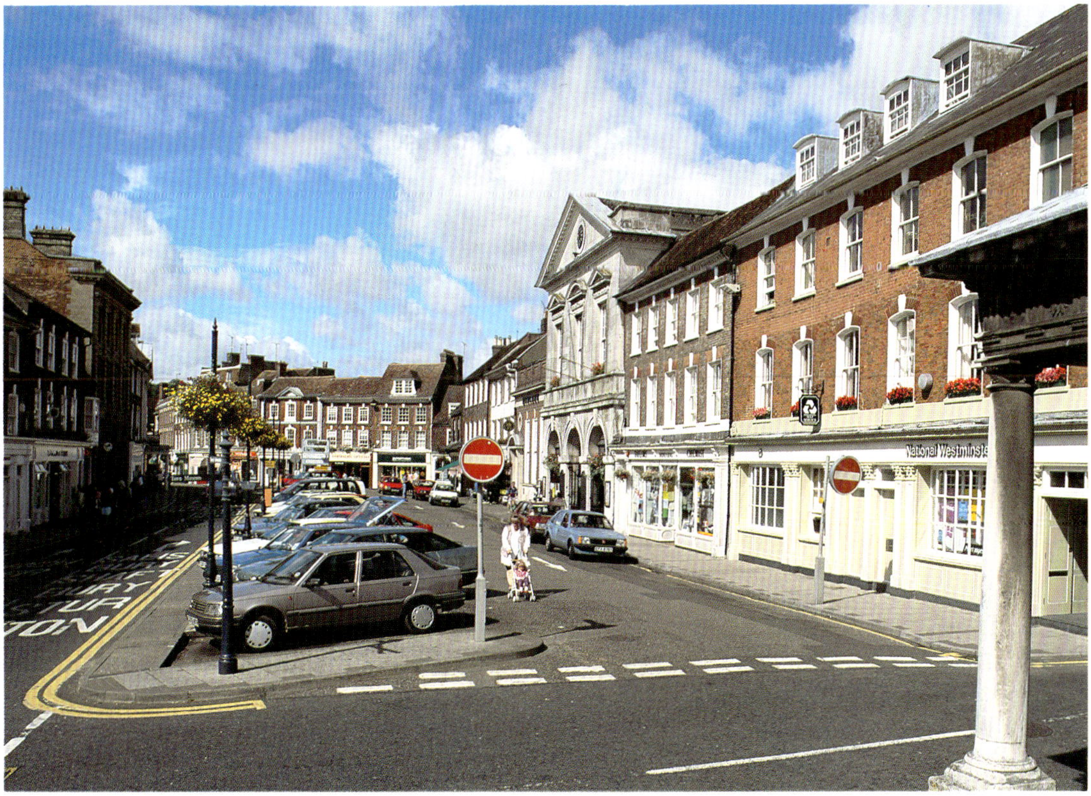

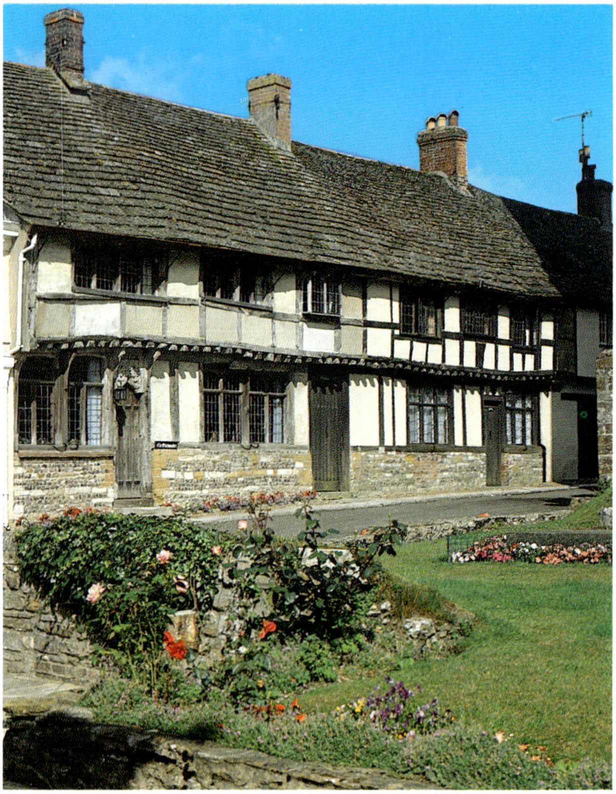

Cottages at Cerne Abbas

Beyond Charminster the road follows the River Cerne to **Cerne Abbas,** a beautiful village of charming old cottages and small period houses. The ruins of the old Abbey founded in memory of Edmund the Martyr in about 987A.D. may be visited.

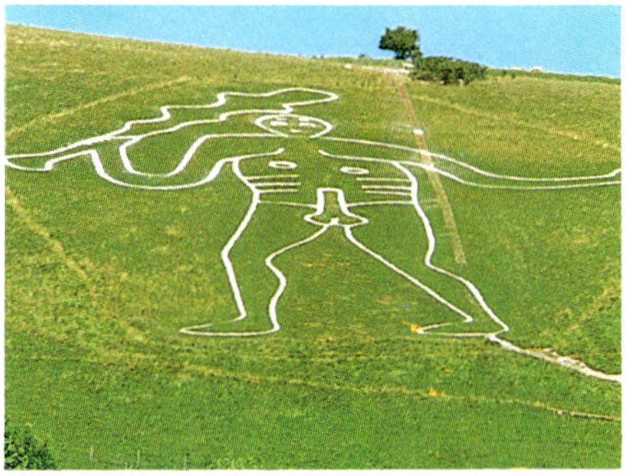

To the north-east of the village of Cerne Abbas is the **Cerne Giant,** a curious figure 180 feet long cut into the chalk hillside. The figure, with club in right hand, is believed to be about 1,500 years old. Of unknown origin, it may be linked with fertility.

Cottages and Church at Milton Abbas

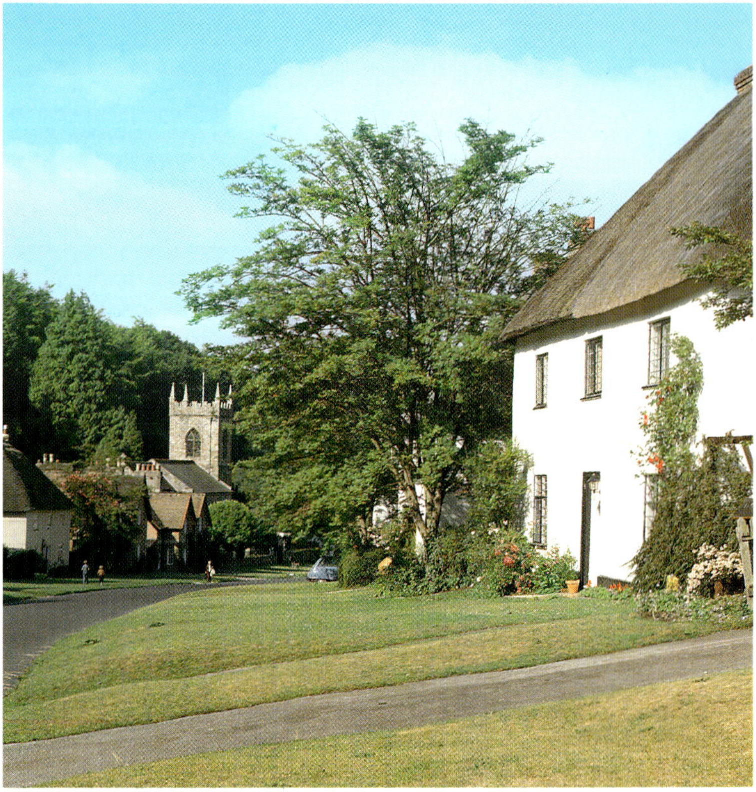

Tiny **Milton Abbas** is a neatly-planned model village with a long curving street lined by thatched cottages. It was created in the 18th century by the Earl of Dorchester when the original village which had grown up during the Middle Ages was levelled to make way for his mansion. The abbey church dates from the 14th century although the Abbey itself is a Benedictine foundation of Saxon origin. Both village and Abbey stand in the midst of peaceful pastoral scenery in a valley which is enclosed by wooded slopes. One of the highest points of the county, Bulbarrow Hill, lies a short distance away to the north west.

Much of the countryside described by Thomas Hardy, one of Dorset's best known literary sons, can still be easily recognised in what has come to be known as **Hardy Country**. In his novels, in which he wrote about the changes which rural areas were facing in the 19th century, Hardy portrayed many features of town and village which remain today. The picturesque thatched cottage in which the author was born still stands at Higher Bockhampton, on the edge of the wild moorland which he called Egdon Heath. The Melstock of "Under the Greenwood Tree" combines features of both Higher and Lower Bockhampton, where Hardy attended the village school, as well as of Stinsford. Here, in the churchyard, Hardy's heart lies buried, surrounded by the Wessex countryside which he loved so much.

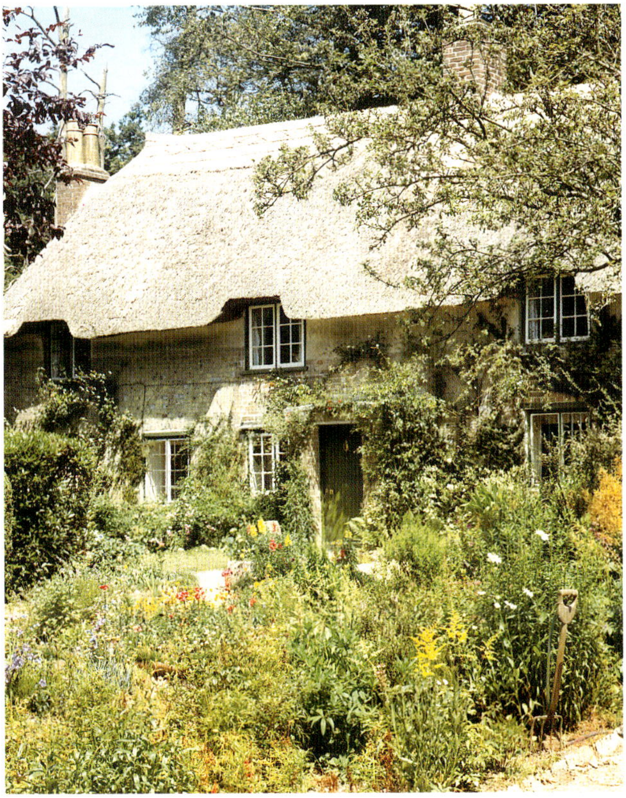

Thomas Hardy's Birthplace, Higher Bockhampton

Stinsford Church

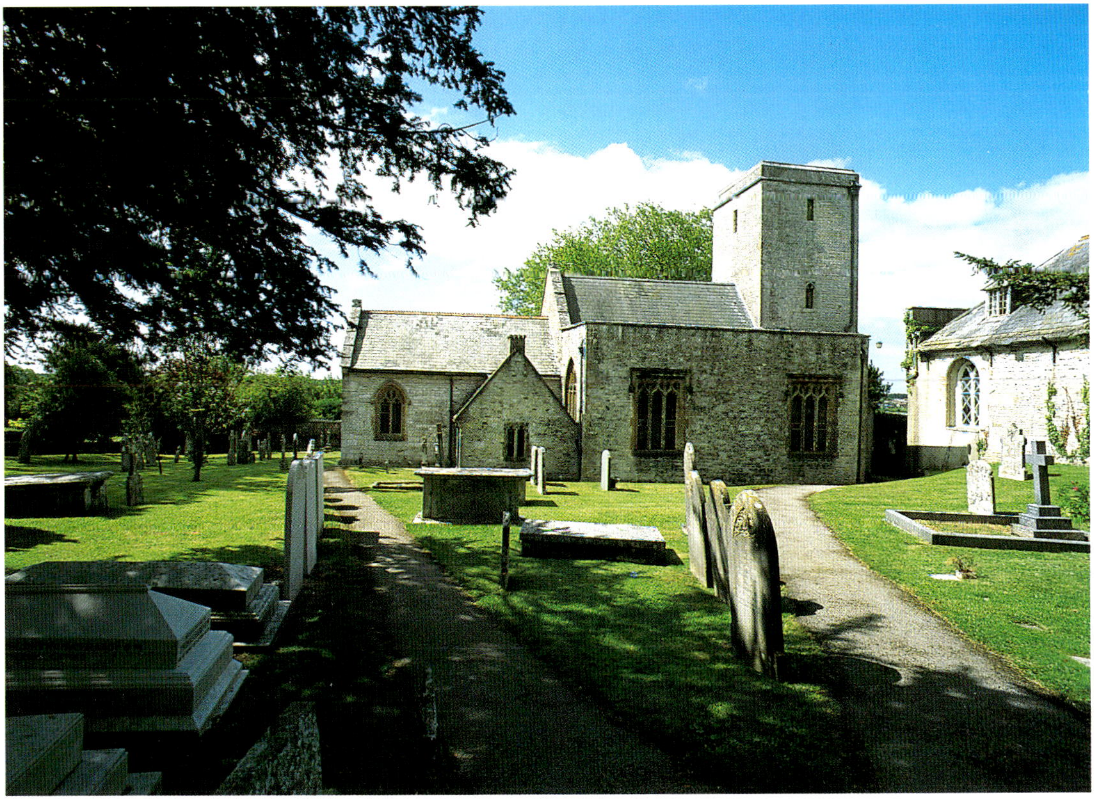

The bustling county town of **Dorchester** is of great historical and archeological interest. It can trace its history back to Saxon times although many of its older buildings were destroyed in a series of fires which occured in the 17th and 18th centuries. The handsome 15th century St. Peter's Church and the Old Shire Hall with its courtroom are among its notable buildings. The impressive Tudor house in the High Street is reputed to have been where the infamous Judge Jeffreys lodged when he held the "Bloody Assizes" in 1685 after the defeat of Monmouth's rebellion. The Keep is an imposing building housing the Dorset Military Museum which contains exhibits relating to local regiments. Dorchester is the town which Thomas Hardy called Casterbridge and many of the buildings which he described in his novels are still standing.

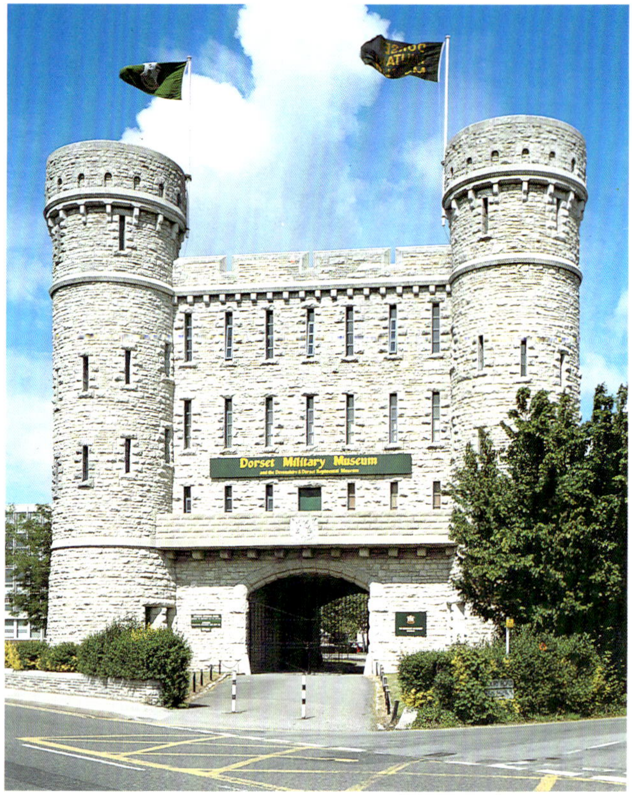

Dorset Military Museum

High West Street, Dorchester

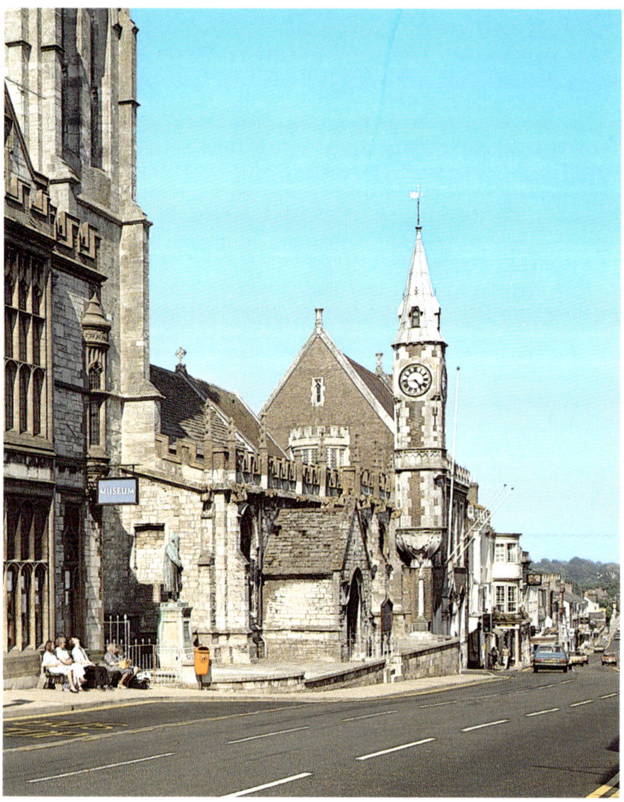

Dominating the landscape around Dorchester is the prehistoric Iron Age hill-fort of **Maiden Castle**. A fortified settlement was probably first built here about 300 BC on the site of a Neolithic village and it is the biggest and most complex fort of its kind in Britain.

Maiden Castle

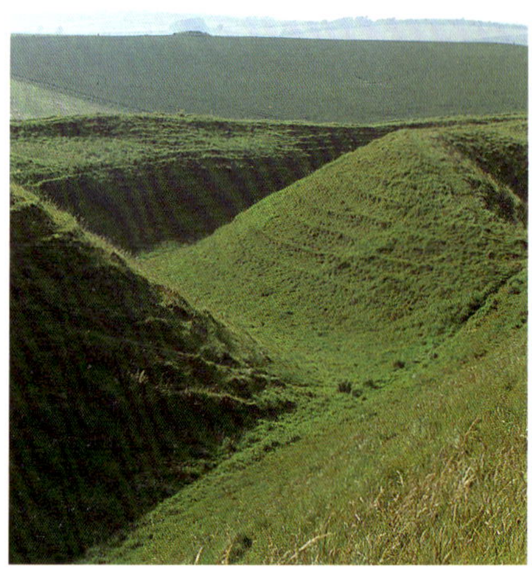